D1281876

The word as image

The word as image

Berjouhi Bowler

Contents

Introduction

The researches into the material for this anthology were begun without a guiding thesis, without a single preconception. Odd doors were knocked on and chance inquiries made into the possibility of locating shaped writing in various cultures. As the material accumulated it became apparent that many of these early picture-texts were in some way connected with magic, ritual, religion or superstition, and that they had an urgency evocative of the LOGOS itself – the incarnated word.

Among the first of the chance discoveries was the pair of Aramaic bowls which appear as endpapers. The texts consist of circular incantations against the evil eye. These bowls were designed to be sunk in the earth at the four corners of a house in order to trap dark spirits and to keep danger from the householder. The demon was supposed to read round the spiral until he reached the centre, and then, unable to read backwards, was caught forever.

The devil trap, with a text so designed that it had magical properties, became the framework and point of reference for all the material later found. And though many shaped texts appearing in the book have not been designed for specifically magical purposes, it is nevertheless fascinating to consider them in such a context.

It has been said that the impulse to wear jewelry grew out of the need to protect the body with amuletic charms. When the literal meaning of the talisman was lost and the magic gone, the amulet became a bauble – aesthetic rather than practical. The texts in this book have been primarily arranged by geographic area beginning in the Far East and ending with the International Concrete Poetry movement. But within these spatial areas the choice of distribution has wherever possible been linked to a progression from amulet to prayer to poem.

Underlying the belief in magic is a faith in the order and uniformity of nature. Elements of chance, accident or caprice do not exist. For the primitive mind each event – wind change, expiring flame, breaking bow – is fraught with suggestion and meaning and the *word* itself is endowed with great power. The Tai peoples from South-east Asia even today tattoo themselves with words to make themselves bullet proof. And the Berber medicine man still writes his healing words into a bowl, washes it with water and gives it to the sick to drink. Fundamental to the success of magic is the belief that change can be caused in conformity with the will. The effectiveness of the amulets and medical prescriptions must depend on the beneficiary's willingness to submit to this persuasion.

Since amulets were originally chosen because of their unusual form or substance, it was not too extraordinary to find that shaped texts were frequently used for protection, healing or for the purposes of control. The diminishing lozenges of the ancient Greeks and Hebrews, the anthropomorphic formulae of the Chinese, the Moroccan amulet in the form of a hand or foot, the Tibetan scorpion charm, all fulfil the demand for the extraordinary. Their full efficacy must be based on the fact that they all have the distinction of the something more – not merely writing, not just a picture but the peculiar combination of both.

It is perhaps this wonder at the extravagance of picture writing, as well as its demands on their ingenuity, which caused so many scribes and calligraphers to shape their prayers in such exotic patterns. In the East, the written word was always felt to be a talisman, and the very process of writing to be a magic art connected not only with the master's technique, skill and art, but also with his spiritual and moral character. The mediaeval outlook made the same stern demands of asceticism on the master calligrapher as it did on members of the religious orders.

Mullah Mir Ali, the Persian calligrapher has said, 'My pen works miracles and rightly enough is the form of my words proud of its superiority over its meaning. To each of the curves of my letters the heavenly vault confesses its bondage in slavery. The value of each of my strokes is eternity itself.'

Writing in the orient was the direct expression of the spirit of man, and for the mystic it was the immediate translation of the vision of the ultimate without the intervention of the objective facts the illustrator was forced to use. But when the calligrapher could combine the Platonic ideal, that writing is the geometry of the spirit, with that most primitive need of all, the urge to make a picture, he must have felt that his offering could satisfy the sternest demands and that his entreaties must be heard.

The curious irony which underlies all the picture texts from the Middle East is the religious injunction in Islam and in Hebraism against the making of images. Most of the specimens from India, Turkey and Persia are in fact verses from the Koran. And the Hebrew texts are mainly drawn into the margins of the Bible. The impulse to make these images then was more powerful than the fear of blasphemy. There is no such prohibition for the Chinese and Japanese calligraphers whose writing was regarded as a collection of symbols used to represent and even evoke all living persons and whose constant search was for a harmony in painting, poetry and calligraphy. This perfect conjunction is best illustrated in the Hokusai painting of Ono-no-Komachi, where the poet's garment is composed of letters making up her name so deftly that it would be impossible for the uninitiated to recognize that the strokes are calligraphic rather than mere drawing.

Apart from the magical and then the mystical impetus to shape texts, poems in the shapes of things – as Boltenhouse[1] calls them – go back as far as the third century BC. The Greeks named such writing technopaegnia. Simias the Rhodean made poems in the shape of an axe, an egg, wings. Dosiadas, his contemporary, made them in the shape of altars. And it is conjectured that there were many such poets among the Alexandrians, not merely the ones collected by Meleager in his *Anthology*. One cannot attribute to these early Greeks or to Apollinaire and Dylan Thomas, who also follow in this tradition, any deep metaphysical properties. But there is little doubt that the immediate effect of a picture poem on the reader is disarming. Resistance is removed. The poem is an offering – a gift immediately accessible as an object. It can be left as a mere picture without further pursuit, like the Communion wafer that is placed on the tongue. It is finally the celebrant's faith and willingness to surrender to the metaphor which will make the spiritual transformation real. So too the reader given the poem as object will spiritualize its contents by his willingness to go on and read.

Most of the art texts included here impose on the reader a rather stern discipline. Simias' egg must be read with the top line first, the bottom line second, the second line from the top third and the second line from the bottom fourth – moving thus from top to bottom and ending with the long line at the centre. The poems of Porfyrius Optatianus are not only to be read horizontally but also along the patterns marked out by the figure. The complicated Turkish ghazal of Shahin Ghiray reads out like the petals of a flower with the centre word acting both as the first and the last word of each line. The Burmese poems again present a nearly insoluble problem for the reader – each figure having its own peculiar key to comprehension.

The reader who persists must attend the work with the force and concentration of re-creation. One might even say that such a study brings with it the rewards of the kind of enlightenment described in the Zen Buddhist proverb 'All things are one when you understand Zen and separate when you do not. All things are one when you misunderstand Zen and separate when you do.' At first one sees a curious picture; then a difficult conundrum is solved as the words are finally understood; and finally the picture once more returns but with renewed understanding. The duality is superseded and the synthesis is made.

The need to leave behind the world of discrete, separated experience, to discard duality, is a characteristic of the mystic's mind. The Tibetan, for example, will not destroy any paper on which a word is written. For him the word and the object are one and the name of a thing is as real as the thing itself. Perhaps this is why the picture poem delights as it does; through its capacity in this small witty way to make a merger and thus represent metaphorically the greater spiritual urge for unity and for the reconciliation of opposites.

It is tempting to conjecture that the reasons for the resurgence of the poem as object in the seventeenth century – the need for more than poetry – by the metaphysical poets Herrick and Herbert, resemble the motives behind the modern movement which is included in the last section of this book. There seems today to be a continually increasing desire to resurrect the Nietzsche-killed father God in the new form of a private dionysiac experience celebrated through the psychiatric insight, the Zen Satori, the psychedelic experiments, various means of arriving at the sense of unity, integration, the all-embracing synthesis.

The baroque age was characterized by excess. The church felt the need to revitalize religious sensibility. The communicant was to be approached through all his senses. He was bombarded with sound – great trumpet canzonas at top volume from both aisles of the cathedral. He was suffused with incense and his eyes fell on great architectural extravagances, streaming fountains, twisting, turning sculptures and paintings, all designed to arouse the failing spirit. Francis Quarles in 1658 wrote in his introduction to his emblem poems, 'And why not shall our blessed Savior be presented to the eye as to the ear? Before the knowledge of letters God was known by his hieroglyphs and emblems of his glory.'

The Dadaist activities in the Cabaret Voltaire – the use of masks, simultaneous poems, silent plays, fracturing of syntax – were an attempt to break down the spectator's expectations and preconceptions: to freshen him and open him up to new diversities and to reintroduce him to a sense of wonder and awe at the force of Creation itself. This is not unlike our current fascination with Artaud theatre, and with large poetry gatherings where masses of people are led by sound poets into reciting random words and parts of words, occasionally going so far as to simulate the trancelike power of speaking a holy mantra. The spectator is thus once again engaged in a vast communal ritual experience, our own version of Baroque religious therapy. The force sought after now is not the omnipotent Judge Who resides outside and above the self to Whom one knelt in submission, but rather the great elemental force within, which we share with each other, and which breaks through our sense of existential alienation and despair.

The International Concrete Poetry movement appears to be based on the need for rehabilitation – not only of the word but of the private individual. Pierre Garnier, a French concrete poet, has said 'Man who is henceforth a cosmic being will have a poetry on the scale of the universe'. And in 1962, in his *Manifesto for a New Poetry – Visual and Phonic* he calls for a world in which the word is coming to be known as a free object. 'It is the task of poets to make the word holy again like the one or two sacred phrases of the Torah.' This statement seems to pull us back to the earlier uses of the word as amulet or as means of deliverance.

Just as the picture poems written in Arabic cover a vast landscape including North Africa, Persia, India and Turkey, (the Hebrew massoretic texts are from Europe as well as the Middle East), so too this current phenomenon is international. Gomringer in his manifesto *From Line to Constellation*, 1954, called the Concrete Poetry movement supranational, suggesting that it is a significant characteristic of the existential necessity of concrete poetry that so much of it appeared simultaneously over Europe and South America. He says, 'I am therefore convinced that concrete poetry is in the process of realizing the idea of a universal poetry.'

Once again the word is to become useful somewhat as were the Persian tughras. Those Koranic verses had a practical function since they were not merely decorative but also amuletic and hung on walls for protective purposes. 'The new poem', says Gomringer, 'is simple and can be perceived visually as a whole as well as in its parts. It becomes an object to be both seen and *used*; an object containing thought but made concrete through play-activity. Its concern is with brevity and conciseness . . . The new reader grasps the idea of play and joins in. In the constellation something is brought into the world. It is a reality in itself and not a poem about something or other. The constellation is an invitation.'

Hans Arp, in 1948, characterized concrete art as an elemental natural healthy art which causes stars of peace, love and poetry to grow in the head and heart. Arp in the 1920s also articulated an idea which was basic to the Dada movement, and which established the path for the concrete poet as well, when he said that the way for the modern was not through the discovery of the perfect form but through submission to the laws of chance which 'embraces all other laws and is as unfathomable to us as the depths from which all life arises. It can only be comprehended by complete surrender to the unconscious.' He maintained that whoever submits to this law attains perfect life.

Stéphane Mallarmé, the acknowledged father of the Concrete Poetry movement, would certainly have agreed with Arp. To him, obsessed by chance as he was, every thought gave off a dice throw. In his now classic 'Un Coup de Dés Jamais N'Abolira le Hasard', written a hundred years ago, we find this concept ingeniously articulated. The words in this peom, which reads across a double page, appear to be cast like dice. They seem to land where they will, in submission to the white spaces of these large pages and are to be read as moving constellations. The images change as the words regroup before our eyes – now reading across, now down, now up. How the words fall looks like an accident, unwilled, without design and without a designer. Implicit to the gesture is the mystic's faith in ultimate meaning and order.

A century later, the French Concretist Jean-Francois Bory might have been describing Mallarmé when he said, 'Concrete writing is real writing only writing writing itself'. The appeal is to non-verbal communication. The concrete poem is designed to be an object in itself, not an interpreter of exterior objects or of subjective feelings, sharing the attributes of a billboard rather than of a lyric poem.

The new poetry is characterized by a vocabulary without boundaries, unstranslatable because it is in its original state immediate and total. There is no explication of text wanted. This is not meant to be a poetry for the cultured few, and the critic as intermediary is merely superfluous. Its guiding impulse is a democratic force, genuine in its desire to approach all men at once and in the same way.

Whether or not some of the examples of concrete included here in the book may be called poetry rather than painting or design is an inevitable question. Since the poet's function traditionally is to separate the word from the stream of continuous talk, stop it and give it fresh existence, we can say that the concrete poet by disassociating the word from its usual setting, breaking it down to syllables, or even by giving us the merest reminiscence of a word, makes us perceive language spoken or written in a way we had not done before. The new word wants nothing to do with personality, psychology or biography. It is even removed from history. The gesture is towards a public word living its own life like a meteor falling through space, aspiring to a pre-humanist anonymity. As has already been said, when the search was begun, there were no conscious assumptions made about the nature of the material which would find its way into the book. As it continued, those texts which seemed to have evocative or aesthetic qualities were kept in and the more ironic and frivolous examples left out. Such familiar patterns as the mouse's tale from Alice in Wonderland or the Rabelais bottle, the eighteenth-century spectacles and frying pan verses, were discarded leaving only the masterful Apollinaire calligram to represent this area, since his poems seem unquestionably to strike the relationship of lyric to shape to tone perfectly and with great freshness.

What did emerge from these researches apart from the immense

diversity and range of picture poems was the archetypal quality of
some of the imagery which occurred and reoccurred in so many
different cultures. Closely wrought mandalas, and endless labyrinths
were common; mythological merged animals – winged serpents,
eagle horses, man-beasts, griffins, unicorns, the ladder, the tree of life.
The fleurs-de-lis were discovered in texts ranging from Malay magic
and ancient Greek Papyri to Hebrew massoretic texts giving one the
sense that the global village existed long before the twentieth century.

An explanation is no doubt possible for all the material in the book
in terms of a basically Western view that there is causality, develop-
ment and progress, that the current phenomena bear some progenitive
resemblance to the past. But equally forceful is the Eastern doctrine of
the moment, summarized by the Arab Jaimi in the fifteenth century:
'experience is discrete not causal, synchronistic and the Universe
consists of accidents pertaining to a single substance which is the
Reality underlying all existences. This universe is changed and
renewed unceasingly at every moment and every breath. Every instant
one universe is annihilated and another resembling it takes its place...
In consequence of this rapid succession, the spectator is deceived into
the belief that the universe is a permanent existence . . . Thus it never
happens that the very being is revealed for two successive moments
under the guise of the same phenomena.'

The book begins and ends with a monument to the dead. The
Egyptian mummy case is buried bandaged in ritual texts from the
Book of the Dead, with words which will safeguard the spirit eternally.
The stone at the end bears mere initials on a block of concrete. It is
just this side of silence and can be seen as the negative but equivalent
regard for the Word.

1 Egyptian inner coffin of Besenmut

消痍化炁符　用酒送下宜發汗

2 Chinese folk amulet

犯坟貼符

3 Chinese talisman

走氣疼符

4 Chinese magic formula

回頭好回頭好世事
將來一筆掃紅塵堆
裏任他忙我心清淨
無煩惱終日貪何時
斷之時身跌倒無常
分明傀儡線牽提線
到沒大小不用金銀
不要賣不分貴賤與
王侯年年多少埋芳
草看看紅日落西山
不覺驀焉天又曉急
回頭莫說早
童易得老才高北斗
富千箱業障隨身何
時了勸世人回頭好
持齋念佛隨身寶看
來名利一場空不如
回頭念佛好

有有無無且耐煩勞碌碌時開人生曲曲灣灣水
世事重重疊疊山古古今今多更變貪貪富富有循環
將將就就隨時過苦苦甘甘命一般

念佛三百聲用硃筆即點一圈點滿共計
十幾萬
生老病死苦人身那個無
若不念彌陀怎得免三途

我見他人死
我心熱如火
不是熱他人
看看輪到我

欲免生死苦
急早念彌陀
生前多念佛
末後生極樂

貪利求名滿世間不如破衲道人間籠雞有食湯鍋近
野鶴無糧天地寬富貴百年難保守輪迴六道易循環
勸君早覓修行路一失人身萬刼難

一盞孤燈照夜臺上床脫了襪和鞋
三魂七魄隨夢轉未知天明來不來

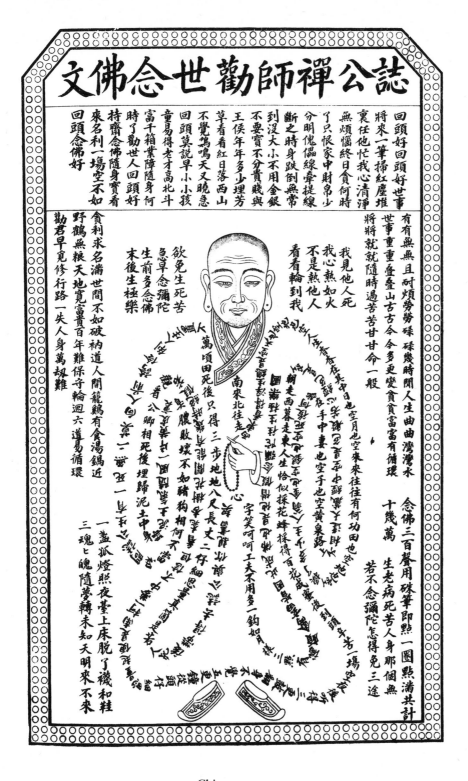

5 Chinese rosary prayer

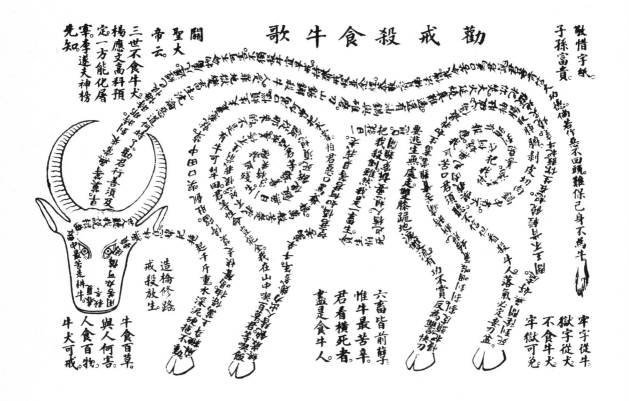

6 Chinese exhortation against killing oxen

7 Chinese stone rubbings

8 Japanese – Zen calligraphy

たのみつゝふかゝらすのみゝゆるかなひとのこゝろのあさくなるさま

せかへしこそのなはしろことくてつくりまつらむ

れゝれてあかしくるよなにはかゝらさこれやひとり

ふなきときみにいひしこといまさらにたをつくり

そしまにもほやきおくまのそでむすびかたくもよそにみゆる

たのみつのふかゝらすのみゝゆるかなひとのこゝろのあさくなるさま

れこしやとのかはたつみうきよとわれはいはせ

もひいてよぬれこしそてのかはらなく

（順集）

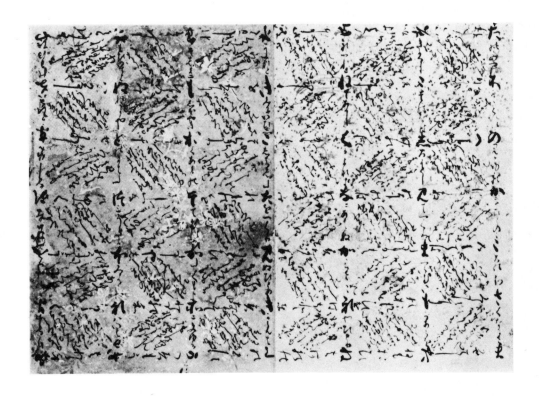

9 Japanese Waka poem

10 Japanese portrait of Ono-no-Komachi

11 Malayan flag of the Sultan of Kalanton

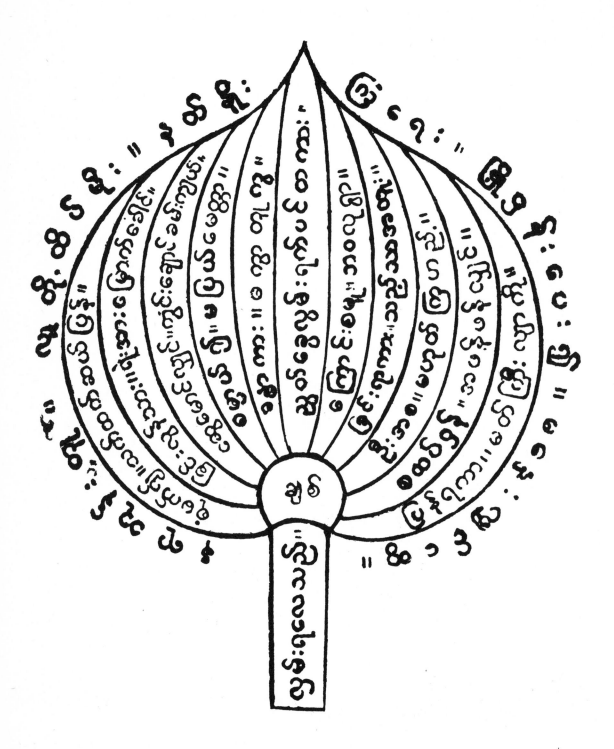

12 Burmese lotus bud writing

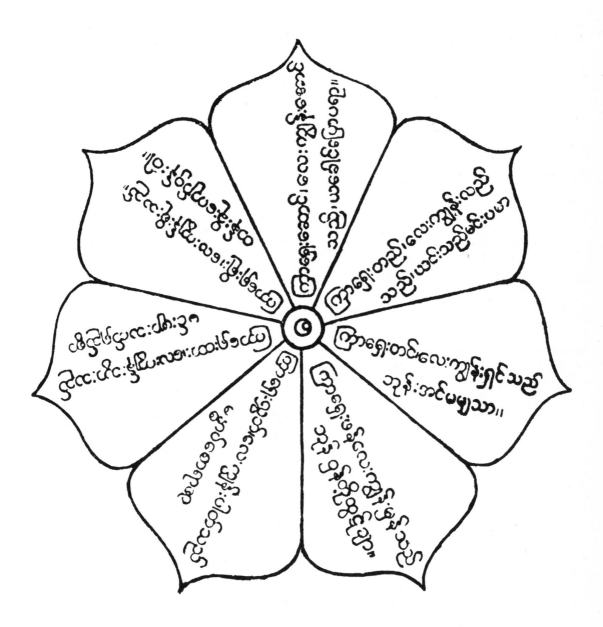

13 Burmese seven wheel jewel writing

14 Tibetan scorpion charm

15 Tibetan. The Tutelary Tam-din's charm

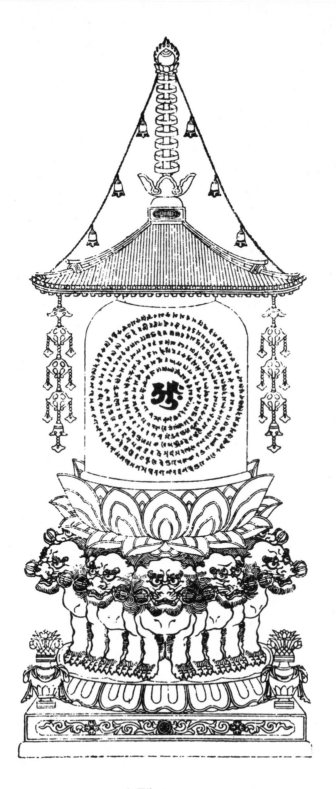

16 Tibetan yantra

17 Tibetan mystic monogram

18 Urdu amulet

19 Indian – symbol for Om

20 Bengali holy vase

21 Indian – Shiva and Annapurna

22 Sanskrit – Hanuman, the monkey-chief

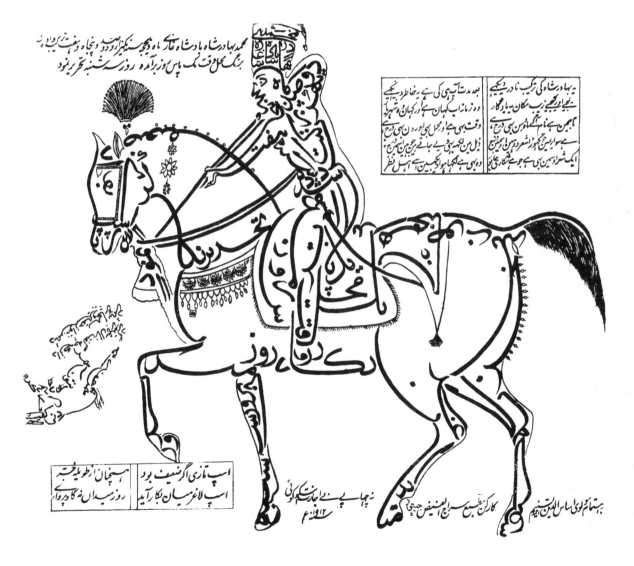

23 Urdu – horse with hunter and hare

24 Urdu – elephant

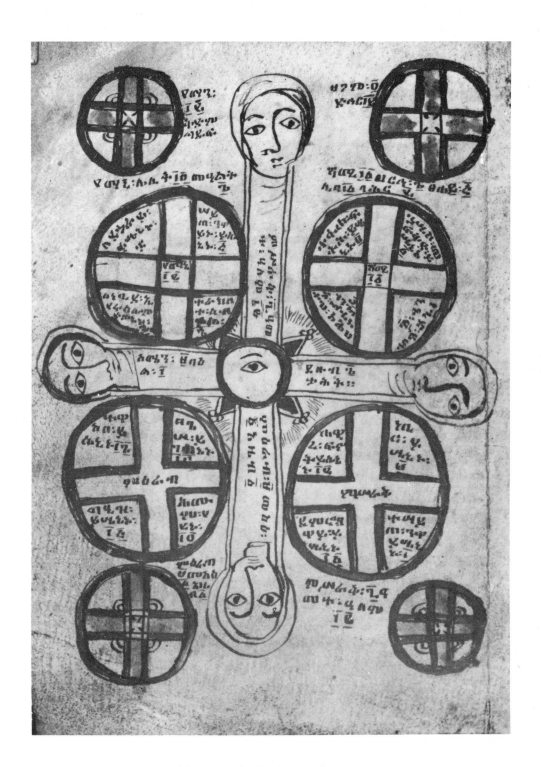

25 Ethiopian medical and magical text

26 Ethiopian medical and magical text

27 Moroccan amulet

28 Persian bird tughra

29 Persian amuletic tughra

30 Persian – invocation to Muhammad

31 Arabic prayer

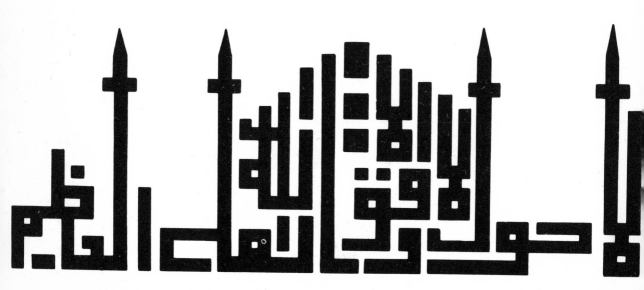

32 Arabic – Kufic script

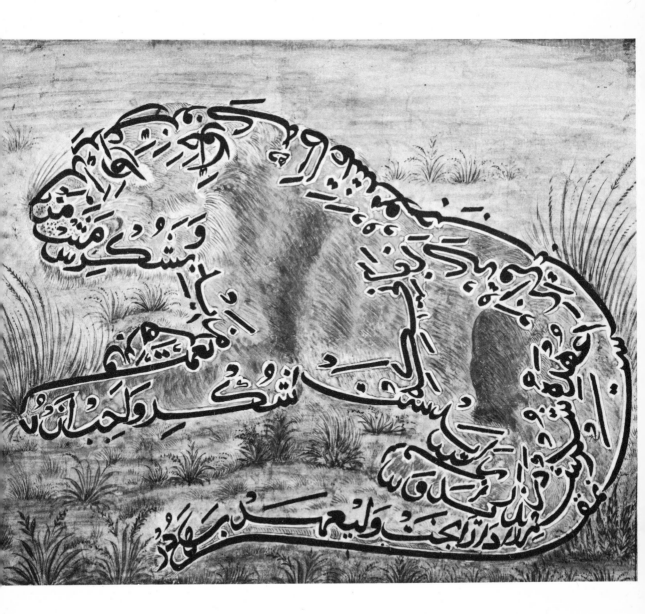

33 Persian prayer

34 Dervish wall hanging

35 Dervish lion

36 Dervish wall hanging

37 Turkish oilcloth chart

38 Turkish double script mosque

39 Turkish figure composed of religious elements

40 Turkish zodiacal man

41 Turkish ghazal or circle ode

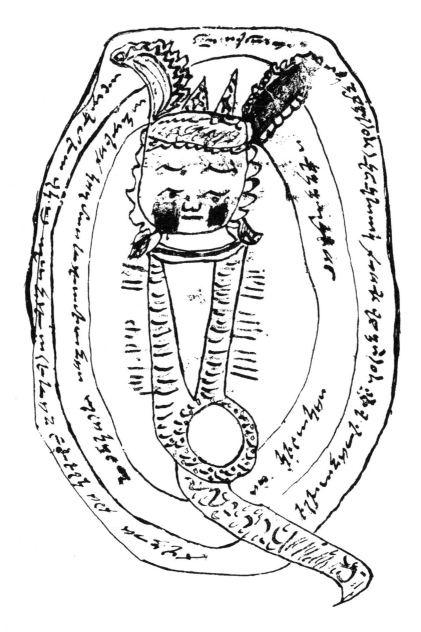

42 Armenian talismanic frontispiece

43 Armenian prayer for mercy

44 Hebrew amulets for childbirth

R.

מעלתו ויבן כל
ישמתו ויאמר
בשמים ממעל

בכל מעשה
בחכמתך ובשמים ד
ישועתך ותהר
באמת כי אתה
ורבך מלכינו אבי
ברוך אתה יי
הארץ מקדש

אתה
יצר כי אתה
נשמה באפו י אלהי
ישראל מלך ומלכותו
בכונותיך והן חלקי
מטובך ומצמיחנו
לעובדך באמ

אמת
לעד
על כל

רצה יי אלהינו בעמך
ובתפלתם שעה י
והשב העבודה לדבי
ישיבת תפלתם מהרה באהבה תקבל ברצון ותהי לרצון
ותמיד עבודת ישראל עמך אנא רחום ברחמיך
השב שכינתך לציון וסדר העבודה לדביר לירושלים
ונעבדך ביראה כימי עולם וכשנים קדמוניות כי
אתה הוא שאתך לבדך ביראה נעבוד מודים אנחנו לך
שאתה הוא יי אלהינו ואלהי אבותינו לעולם ועד
צור חיינו מגן ישענו אתה הוא לדור
ודור נודה לך ונספר תהלתך על
חיינו המסורים בידך ועל נשמות
תפקידות לך ועל נסיך שבכל יום
עמנו ועל נפלאותיך וטובותיך
שבכל יום עת ערב ובקר וצהרים הטו
כי לא כלו רחמיך והמרחם כי לא תמו חסד
כי מעולם קוינו לך ועל כולם יתברך ויתרומם
תמיד שמך מלכינו לעולם ועד אבינו מלכי
זכור רחמיך וכבש כעס מעלינו
דבר וחרב ורעב ושבי ועון ומשחית ומגפה מעלינו

ימעל כל
ומתוצלהי
בני בריתך
יברך
ברוך אתה יי

בני בריתך
טובם כל
וכל החיים
סלה
טוב
הטוב טמ

46 Hebrew massoretic text

47 Hebrew massoretic text

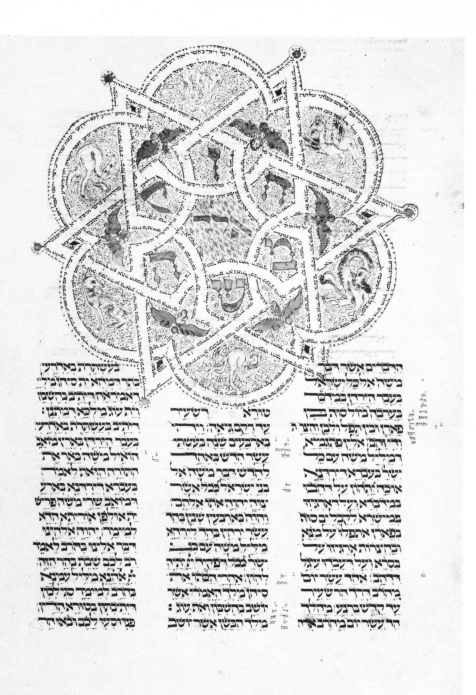

48 Hebrew massoretic text

49 Hebrew massoretic text

50 Hebrew massoretic text

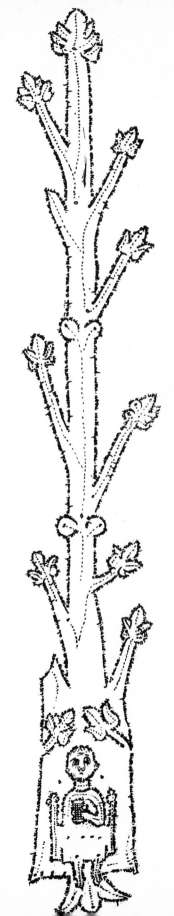

51 Hebrew massoretic text – Jonah beneath the gourd

אמה ..א כתי' הא' בלשין פעירטא וסימ' אמה יל ובר בנו רמילכים
רתמיד דיגעעמד אנה ל' ציל בגן פארבריה . חלתאג ות דברי ער וחיהי
אמה יל בילשין במשרי . צנה יל כי צנו עלדר : וכל לשין . אושי יצ
רצומתקן : ם ברוקה ד' חל . וכי ם ברייהה ער צצר . פרחה מתר . ה

52 Hebrew massoretic text – Jonah and the whale

53 Hebrew massoretic text

Ἀβρασαξ ιαεωβαφρενεμουνοθιλαρικριφιαευεαιφιρκιραλιθονυομενερφαβωεαι Βαινχωωωχ

ωυοιηεα αεωβαφρενεμουνοθιλαρικριφιαευεαιφιρκιραλιθονυομενερφαβωεα αεηιουω Δαμναμενευ

υοιηεαω εωβαφρενεμουνοθιλαρικριφιαευεαιφιρκιραλιθονυομενερφαβωε εηιουωα αμναμενευ

οιηεαωυ ωβαφρενεμουνοθιλαρικριφιαευεαιφιρκιραλιθονυομενερφαβω ηιουωαε μναμενευ

20 ιηεαωυο βαφρενεμουνοθιλαρικριφιαευεαιφιρκιραλιθονυομενερφαβ ιουωα[εη ναμενευ 20

ηεαωυοι Ιαω αφρεν[εμου]νοθιλαρικριφιαευεαιφιρκιραλιθονυομενερφα ουωα[εηι ω αμενευ

εαωυοιη Ιαω φρεν[εμο]υνοθιλαρικριφιαευεαιφιρκιραλιθονυομενερφ υωαεη[ιο υω μενευ

αωυοιηε ιωια ρενεμ[ο]υνοθιλαρικριφιαευεαιφιρκιραλιθονυομενε ιαωαωι ωαεηιου ουω ενευ

αιωιαω ιιι ααα ω ενεμ[ου]νοθιλαρικριφιαευεαιφιρκιραλιθονυομενε

25 ωω ιιι οοο υυυ ωωω νεμ[ου]νοθιλαρικριφιαευεαιφιρκιραλιθονυομεν ωια αιω ιαω ιιι ααα ιουω νευ 25

ωια αωι αιω ωια ω ια εμ[ου]νοθιλαρικριφιαευεαιφιρκιραλιθονυομε ηωω ωιιιι οοο υυυ ωω

ιιι ααα εεε ηηη ιιιιι οοοο μου]νοθιλαρικριφιαευεαιφιρκιραλιθονυομ ψιạιψị ạιψ ψιạωιạ[ω] ηιουω ευ

ο γγγγγ ψψψ ψψψψ ου]νοθιλαρικριφιαευεαιφιρκιραλιθονυο ιιι ααα εεε ηηη ιιιι οο[ο]ο εηιουω υ

αβλαναθαναλβα υ]νοθιλαρικριφιαευεαιφιρκιραλιθονυ ο υυυυ ωωωωωωω[ω] αεηιουω

30 βλαναθαναλβα νοθιλαρικριφιαευεαιφιρκιραλιθον ακραμμαχαμαρι

λαναθαναλβα οθιλαρικριφιαευεαιφιρκιραλιθο κραμμαχαμαρι

αναθαναλβα θιλαρικριφιαευεαιφιρκιραλιθ ραμμαχαμαρι

ναθαναλβα ιλαρικριφιαευεαιφιρκιραλι α αμμαχαμαρι

αθαναλβα λαρικριφιαευεαιφιρκιραλ εε μμαχαμαρι

35 ω θαναλβα α αρικριφιαευεαιφιρκιρα ηηη μαχαμαρι

υω αναλβα ε]α ρικριφιαευεαιφιρκιρ ιιιι αχαμαρι

ουω ναλβα η ε]α ικριφιαευεαιφιρκι οοοοο χαμαρι

ιουω αλβα ιη ε]α κριφιαευεαιφιρκ υυυυυυ αμαρι

ηιουω λβα οιηεα ριφιαευεαιφιρ υωωωωω μαρι

40 εηιουω βα υοιηεα ιφιαευεαιφι ααααααα αρι

αεηιουω α ωυοιηεα φιαευεαιφ εεεε]εε ρι

ιαευεαι ηηηη]η ι

αευεα [ιιιι]

ευε οο]ο

υ υυ

ω

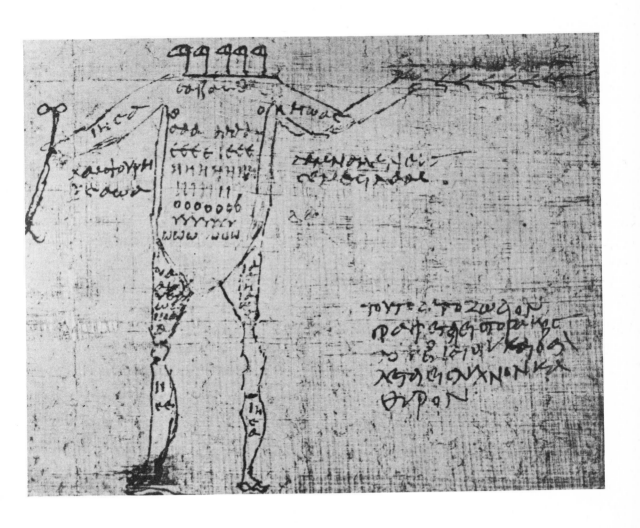

55 Greek magical papyrus – decapitated god

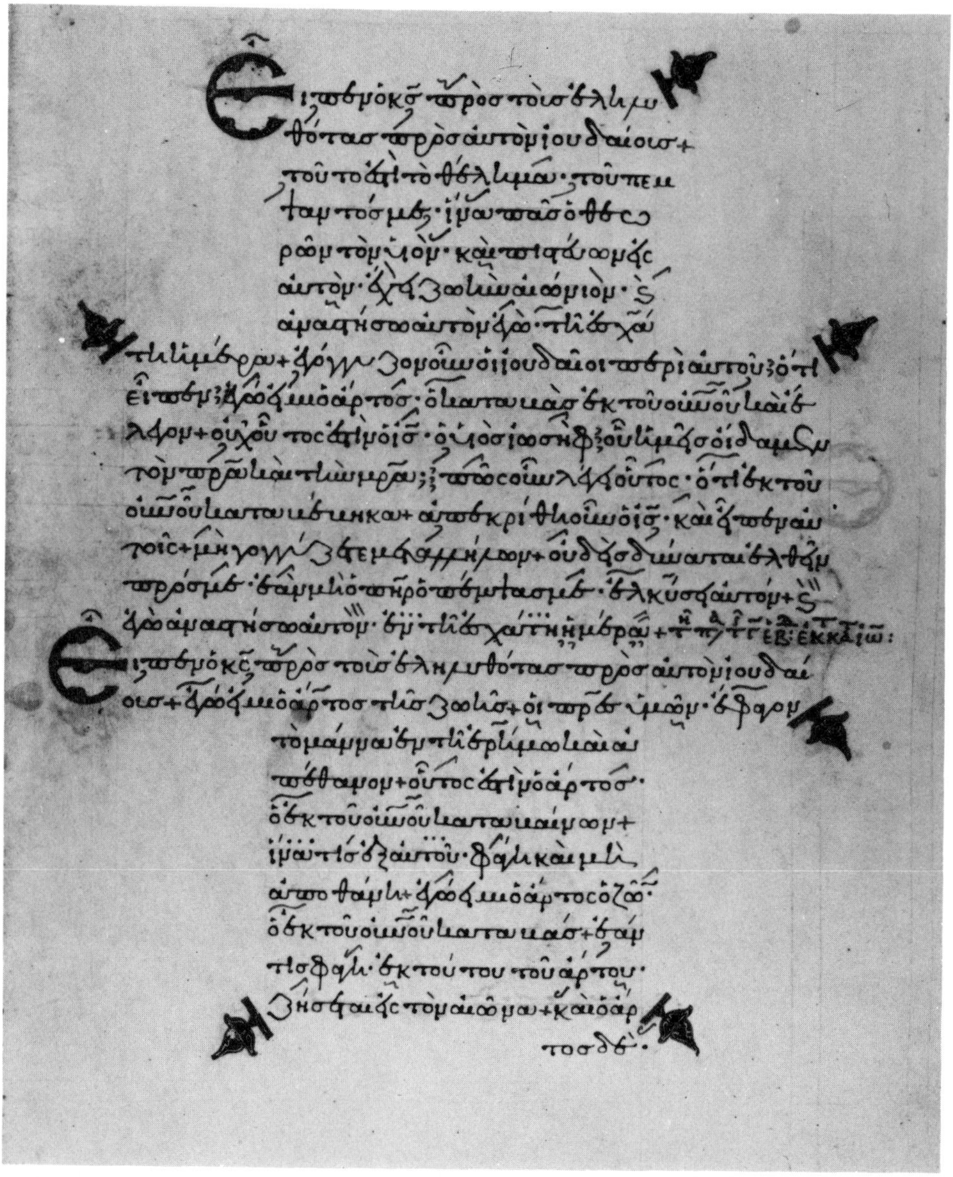

56 Greek – cross from an Evangelestarium

Κωτίλας
τῇ τόδ᾽ ἄτριον νέον
πρόφρων δὲ θυμῷ δέξο· δὴ γὰρ ἁγνᾶς
τὸ μὲν θεῶν ἐριβόας Ἑρμᾶς ἔκιξε κάρυξ
ἄνωγε δ᾽ ἐκ μέτρου μονοβάμονος μέγαν πάροιθ᾽ ἀέξειν
θοᾶς δ᾽ ὕπερθεν ὦκα λέχριον φέρων νεῦμα ποδῶν σποράδων πίφαυσκεν
θοαῖς ἴσ᾽ αἰόλαις νεβροῖς κῶλ᾽ ἀλλάσσων ὀρσιπόδων ἐλάφων τέκεσσιν
πᾶσαι κραιπνοῖς ὑπὲρ ἄκρων ἱέμεναι ποσὶ λόφων κατ᾽ ἀρθμίας ἴχνος τιθήνας
καί τις ὠμόθυμος ἀμφίπαλτον αἶψ᾽ αὐδὰν θὴρ ἐν κόλπῳ δεξάμενος θαλαμᾶν μυχοιτάτῳ
κλ.τ᾽ ὦκα βοᾶς ἀκοὰν μεθέπων. δ γ᾽ ἄφαρ λάσιον νιφοβόλων ἀν᾽ ὀρέων ἔσσυται ἄγκος
ταῖσι δὴ δαίμων κλυτᾶς ἴσα θοοῖς δονέων ποσὶ πολύπλοκα μετίει μέτρα μολπᾶς
ῥίμφα πετρόκοιτον ἐκλιπὼν ὕρους᾽ εὐνάν, ματρὸς πλαγκτὸν μαιόμενος βαλίας ἐλεῖν τέκος
βλαχαὶ δ᾽ οἴων πολυβόταν ἀν᾽ ὀρέων νομὸν ἔβαν τανυσφύρων ἐς ἀν᾽ ἄντρα Νυμφῶν
ταὶ δ᾽ ἀμβρότῳ πόθῳ φίλας ματρὸς ῥώοντ᾽ αἶψα μεθ᾽ ἱμερόεντα μαζὸν
ἴχνει θένωι . . . τὰν παναίολον Πιερίδων μονόδουπον αὐδὰν
ἀριθμὸν εἰς ἄκραν δεκάδ᾽ ἰχνίων κόσμον νέμοντα ῥυθμῶν
φῦλ᾽ ἐς βροτῶν, ὑπὸ φίλας ἐλὼν πτεροῖσι ματρός
λίγειά μιν κάμ᾽ ἶφι ματρὸς ὠδὶς
Δωρίας ἀηδόνος
ματέρος.

Ολός ὔ με λιβρὸς ἱρῶν
Λιβάδεσσιν, οἷα κάλχη,
Ὑπὸ Φοινίησι τέγγει·
Μαύλιες δ᾽ ὕπερθε πέτρης Ναξίας θούμεναι
Παμάτων φίδοντο Πανός· οὐ στροβίλῳ λιγνύϊ
Ἰξὸς εὐώδης μελαίνει τρεχνέων με Νυσίων.
Ἐς γὰρ βωμὸν ὁρῆς με, μήτε γ᾽ αὐροῦ
Πλίνθοις, μήτ᾽ Ἀλύβης παγέντα βώλοις·
Οὐδ᾽ ὃν Κυνθογενὴς ἔτευξε Φύτλη
Λαβὼν τὰ μηκάδων κέρα,
Λισσαῖσιν ἀμφὶ δειράσιν
Ὅσσαι νέμονται Κυνθίας,
Ἰσόρροπος πέλοιτό μοι.
Σὺν Οὐρανοῦ γὰρ ἐκγόνοις
Εἰνάς. μ᾽ ἔτευξε γηγενής·
Τάων δ᾽ ἀείζωον τέχνην
Ἔνευσε πάλμυς ἀφθίτων.
Σὺ δ᾽ ὦ πιὼν κρήνηθεν, ἣν
Ἶνις κόλαψε Γοργόνος,
Θύοις τ᾽ ἐπισπένδοις τέ μοι
Ὑμηττιάδων πολὺ λαροτέρην
Σπονδήν· ἄδην ἴθι δὴ θαρσέων
Ἐς ἐμὴν τεῦξιν· καθαρὸς γὰρ ἐγὼ
Ἰὸν ἱέντων τεράων, οἷα κέκευθ᾽ ἐκεῖνος
Ἀμφὶ Νέαις Θρηικίαις, ὃν σχεδόθεν Μυρίνης
Σοί, Τριπάτωρ, πορφυρέου Φὼρ ἀνέθηκε κριοῦ.

In hac pagina dextrorsu scripta a monogramma ihu ortu principiu lectionis ut pectore
levet obscuritas. In qua duo usus grece s incipientes a leva parte monogrami er qb unus
eide signi   reliquis partib funct media litera ß terminatur. ΤΗΝ ΗΑΥΝΑΕΥΚΕ ΧΟ
ΝΥΑΕ ΑΡΧΕΝΟΗΕ ΙΝΟΘΕΙΖΙΝ ΔΙΕ inde descendens ad alueu nauis spem gubnaculi par-
tis sue fine eecludit q est talis. ΟΫ ΡΟΙΕΤΕΙΝ ΟΧΕΝΙΟΗΙΕΕ ΕΑΡΕΤΕ ΕΑΝΕΝΟΙΕ. Versus vq aut
apra incipiut aut arostro aut a remis aut de sub pra ettremo puppis acumine tminati
tertia uice alia uota eecludit q se tales. Nauta ne tutus eeminat suine pellas ß Higias ue
tutus eenat summus cumulata ephes ß Pulsa mente mala eenat suine procellas.
ß Spe q roma bona eenat suine pellas. ß Roma felix floret semiper uotis T V I S ⚬

```
P R O D E V N T V R . M I H I L O C A E L E S T I A S I E H A L E G E N T I
C O N S T A N T I N E D E C V S . M V N D I L V X A V R E A S A E C L I
Q V I S . T V A M I X T A C A N A T M I R A P I E T A T E T R O P H A E A
A E M V L I A Q V A M . C L A V H C . C . G E H L T O R I S . C A L L I O P E A E
C O M P O S V I T A L L H V H C O H S . P E R F V S A L I Q V O R E
V E R S I F I C A S . H E L I C O H I H . G A V D I A P R O I V A T V M D A S
C I E M E N T I Q V E H O V V H V O E H . D E P E C T O R E V E R S O .
H A O Q V E E G O . M A G N A H I O L D I C A M . H V M E R O S A C A H E H D O
S C E P T R A D V C I S . O X Z A T . H O B L S . V A T G R A E C I A D O H A
S A E C L A Q V E B I E O N I L C O S O C I A L L I M I T E F I R M A S .
R O M V L A L V X . C O H D I A H O V I S . F L O R E H T I A V O T I S
V O T O S C A I P T A C A H O A L L O A R S . C A H V I N E I E C T O .
I A O B E L L I S . T O T V O H Y S C V O . P R A P L E C T E R E C L V E O .
V T R E A T R V B I . C O H . P A E I L L P E T I I A E T H E R A I V H E
H V H C F E L I X P H O P R I O S . P A R I S . O E S C R V P E A V I S V S .
I A M S T I M V L A T S I G H I S . E X V L T A N S . O V S A H O T A R E
G A V D I A L A E T V S . H V M C P E R V O E H O T A Z I H V I A P H O E B V S .
H E I I T O . P O O Q V B E R T A O V O C A H E L A V R E A P I P E C T H O .
A H T E V O T I S . P I C T A F E L I C I A S . A E C V I A P I A V D E H S .
S I C A E S T V S . V A T I S . F I D O D V C E P I T H I A E C A R V E H S .
H V H C . T V T V S . C O H T E O H A T . S V M M E P R O C A R E D O V E R O .
H V H C M A R E S I G A E V O . V A L E A M B V E F R A H E E R E R E M O .
C A R B A S A H O C T I G E R O V O T O T V O S I . S C R V P E A T E H D O .
P V L B I T A D E P O R T A H S . V I S A H C O H T E X E R H A V E O I
O V S A S I H I T C O H V H C T A T V O . S P E S . I H C I L I T A V O T O .
M E H T E O P E R T O R T V O F E S S A O H O H . F R A M O L A T H I V L E O .
I A V S . M E A . F I C T A P V E S T A H S . O A G H A O O E H O E H D O
S I G H A P A I A H D I C A O I A E T I S . S I O A F I V O I H A S A H C T V
O E H T E B O H A C O H T E O H A T . S V M O I S . C V O S I B L A G O H E O I
V O T I S . P O S T F R V C T V O O A R T E O . C L E M E H T I A R E D V E T .
S I C H O R A S . I E C T O T V O . C R E S C V H T A V R E A S A E C L A .
O O R T A L I O V I H C E H S . I A O B L S . V I C E H H I A R E D D E S .
C A R O L H A O V A E . P I C T A S . O I L R D . D E H O O I H E F O R O E T
F L O R E H O T A H S . V O T V O . V A R I O . D A T P A G I H A F E L I X
A V G V S T A E S O D O L I S . O E O O R A H S . I H S I G H I A F A T A
I V D I C E T E V E L . T E S T E P I O . C O H D I O H A P A R E H T I S .
I V H G E H T V R T I . T V I I S . F E L I C I A F A C T A H E P O T V O I
```

PRODENTVRMINIOCAELESTIASIGNALEGENTI
CONSTANTINEDECVSMVNDILVXAVREASAECLI
QVISTVAMIXTACANATMIRAPIETATETROPAEA
EXVLTANSDVXSVMMENOVISMEAPAGINAVOTIS
AEMVLAQVAMCLARIIGENITORISCALLIOPEAE
COMPOSVITTALINVNCMENSPERFVSALIQVORE
VERSIFICASHELICONINGAVDIAPROFLVATVNDAS
CLEMENTIQVENOVVMNVMENDEPECTOREVERSET
NAMQVEEGOMAGNANIMIDICAMNVMEROSACANENDO
SCEPTRADVCISGAZZAENOBISDATGRAECIADONA
SAECLAQVEBLEMMYICOSOCIALILIMITEFIRMAS
ROMVLALVXCONDIGNANOVISFLORENTIAVOTIS
VOTOSCRIPTACANOOALIMARSCARDINETECTO
IAMBELLISTOTVMMYSEVMPERPLECTERECIVEM
VTPATEATRVBICONPARILIPETITAETHERAIVRE
NVNCFELIXPROPRIOSPACISMESCRVPEAVISVS
IAMSTIMVLATSIGNISEXVLTANSMVSANOTARE
GAVDIALAETVSNVNCPERMENOTATAVIAPHOEBVS
RETITOQVOQVETEXTANOVOCANELAVREAPLECTRO
ARTENOTISPICTAFELICIASAECVLAPLAVDENS
SICAESTVSVATISFIDODVCEPYTHIECARPENS
NVNCTVTVSCONTEMNATSVMMEPROCANEGOVERO
NVNCMARESIGAEVMVALEAMBENEFRANGEREREMO
CARBASANOCTIFERVMTOTVMSISCRVPEATENDO
PVLPITADEPORTANSVISAMCONTEXERENAVEM
MVSASINITCONIVNCTATVOSPESINCLITAVOTO
MENTEMPERTORTVMFESSAMNONFRANGATHIVLCO
LAVSMEAFICTAPEDESTANSMAGNAMOLEDOCENDI
SIGNAPALAMDICAMLAETISSIMAFLVMINESANCTO
MENTEBONACONTEMNATSVMMISCVMSIBIAGONEM
VOTISPOSTFRACTVMMARTEMCLEMENTIAREDDET
SICNOBISLECTOQVOCRESCVNTAVREASAECLA
MOXLATIOVINCENSIAMBISVICENNIAREDDES
CARMINEQVAEPIETASMIRODENOMINEFORMET
FLORENOTANSVOTVMVARIODATPAGINAFELIX
AVGVSTAESOBOLISMEMORANSINSIGNIAFATA
IVDICETEVELTESTEPIOCONDIGNAPARENTIS
IVNGENTVRTITVLISFELICIAFACTANEPOTVM

60 Latin – 'Carmina Figurata', modern setting

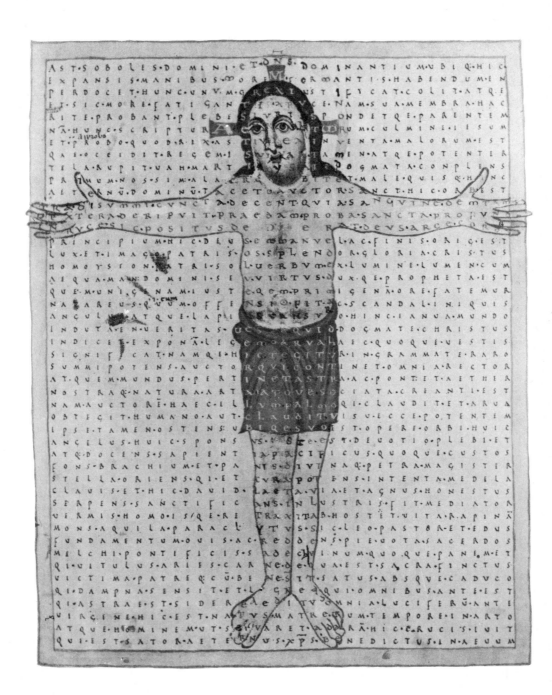

61 Latin 'Christ on the Cross'

62 Latin – Lamb of God and four apocalyptic symbols

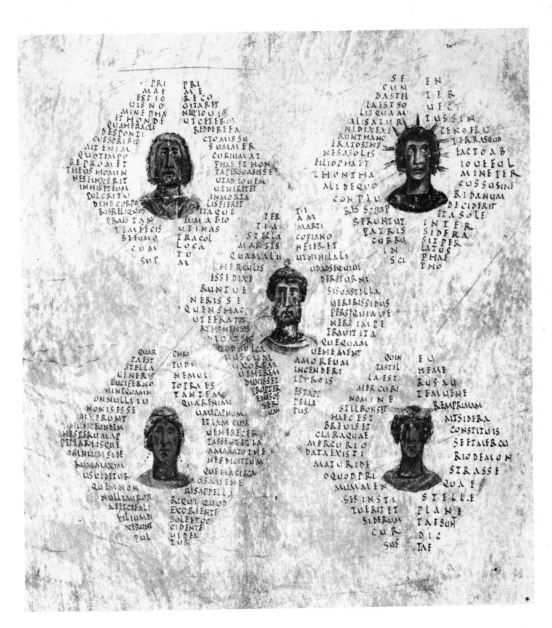

63 Latin – Aratus' *Phaenomena*

64 Latin – Aratus' *Phaenomena*, Perseus

65 Latin – Aratus' *Phaenomena*, Cygnus

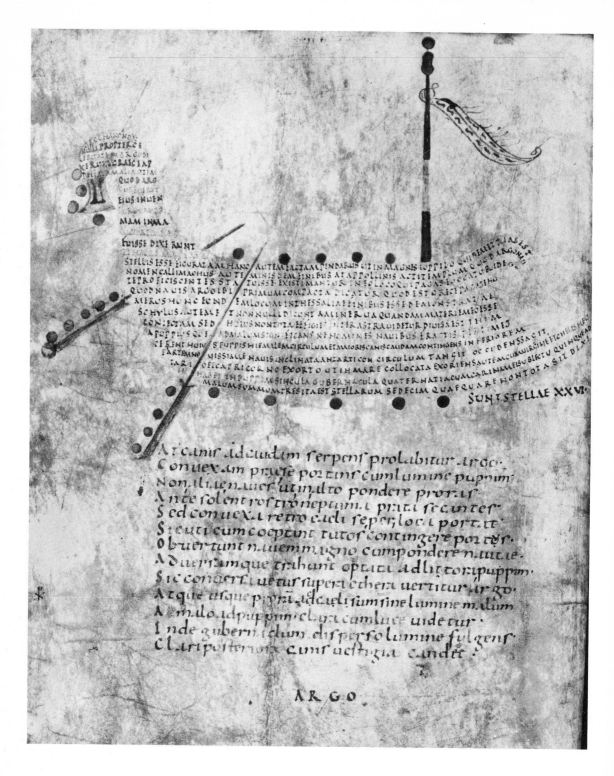

STELLIS ESSE FIGURAI A CUHANC AUTEM A CT A A CLPINDASIS OT IN MAGNIS TOPPIS TO QUISBELLE MAS LS T
NOMEN CALLIMACHUS AUTEM MINIS SEM FINI BUS AT APPOLLINIS ACTITI AMPTANUM G O ED ARGOMIL
TETRO FICISENTES STAT UISSE EXISTIMANTUR IN SOLO COQ UT PAJAS I GC CATUR IDES
QUOD NAUIS ARGO IBI PRIAM UM COMPACTA DICATUR Q UOD EST GORETI A RSENO
ATERIS HUNC SCND EM LOCO M UT IN THESSALIA E FINI BUS ESSE D EA MOST RAT AL
SCHVLUS AUTEM E T NON NULLI DICUNT AAC INERUA QUANDAM ALATERI S EMEDISSE
CONIETAM SED HUIUS NON ITA HI FIGIE IN TERA ST RA UI DETUR PLUISA ES T HI AI
A PUPPIS QUE E ABMALU M SIQ IN EICANS NF HOMINES NAUI BUS ERA TIS PERI TIMES
CE SENT HON S PUPPIS HI FI AMA LEM EICIRCULUM ET MAIORIS CANIS CAUDAM CONTIGHENS IN FERIOREM OC CIDENS SACIT
PARTEM NO MISSI ACLE HAUIS INCLINATA ANTARTI CON CIRCULUM TANGIT AUCH LIRCHIETE HELISHES
TAR T O ECAP RICOR NO EXORTO UT IN MARE COLLOCATA EXORIENS AUTEM ACURIN UM LEIS U BIETU QUI HOEAD
HASEI IN PUPP MOSIHCULA GUBERNHACULA QUATER HATIA CUM CARINA MEIS U BIET DIXI
MALUM SUMMUM TRES ITA EST STELLARUM SEDECIM QUA FQUARE HONT OIA SIT Q SUNT STELLAE XXVI

A r canis adcaudem serpens prolabitur Argo.
Conuexam prae se portat cumlumine puppim·
Non illi uenauer ut in ulto pondere proraif·
Ante solent rostro neptuni a prati secantes·
Sed conuexa retro caeli seper loca portat·
Si cutir cum coeptint tutos contingere portes·
Obuertunt nauem magno cum pondere nautae·
Aduersamque trahunt optata ad littori puppim·
Sic conuertitur super aethera uertitur Argo·
Atque usque priri ad caeli lumine lumine malium
A malo id puppim clara cumluce uidetur·
Inde gubernaclum disperso lumine fulgens
Claripostenota cunis uestigia candit·

ARGO·

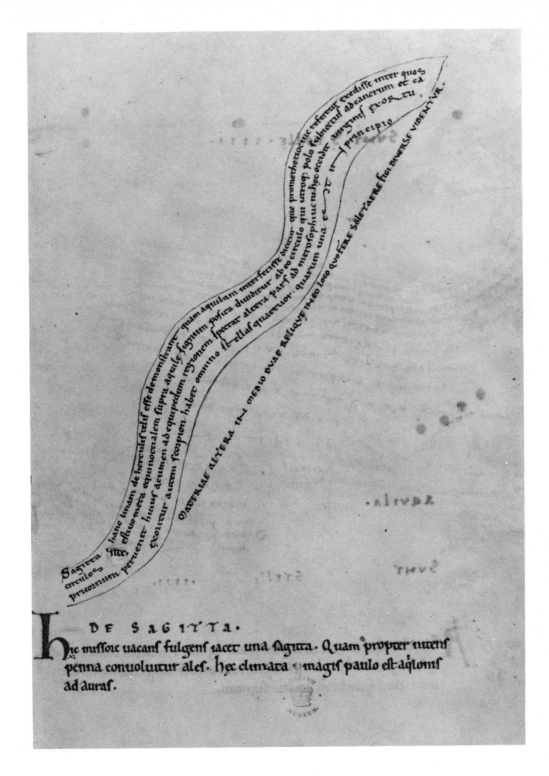

DE SAGITTA·

Hic missile uacans fulgens iacet una sagitta· Quam propter nitens
penna conuoluitur ales· Hec climata ꞓmagis paulo est aꝙlonis
ad auras.

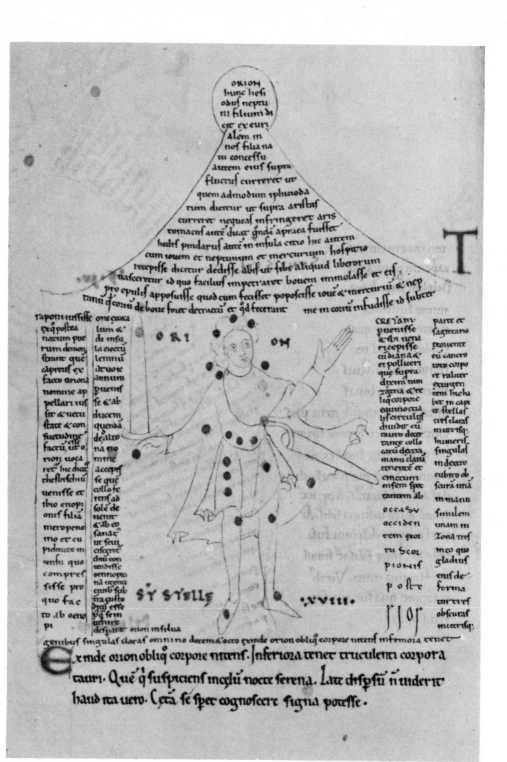

69 German gothic calligram

70 English – The Ten Commandments

"Ecce beato S.

Lux nos dedisse maximE,

Illustris illa credituR,

Sēpiterno quæ celebrāda cultV,

Anglia, insigni generata stirpE,

Beata virgo cum regnare cæperaT ;

Eam parem patulæ dixeris arborI ;

Tempestate gravi subito ruentE

Huius se foliis tegunt volucreS,

Adeuntq. bruta procubitV

Magnū iuvamen omnibuS

Regina princeps: profugI

Eius celebrāt nomeN :

Gentibus ipsa laC,

Inclyta, virgO,

Non negat, iis simuL

Alma nutrix manV

Miserit auxiliuM.

Det deus itaquE

Impleat annuM.

Vivat & integrA,

Nullibi vnquam deficiens supremuM

Omnibus auxilium, quæ exhibuit piE

BIS locupletur ô patriæ columeN."

This   cross-tree   here
Doth   JESUS   beare,
Who   sweet'ned   first,
The   death   accurs't.

HERE all things ready are, make hast, make hast away;
For, long this work wil be, & very short this day.
Why then, go on to act: Here's wonders to be done,
Before the last least sand of Thy ninth hour be run;
Or e're dark clouds do dull, or dead the mid-dayes sun.

Act when Thou wilt,
Bloud will be spilt;
Pure balm, that shall
Bring health to all.
Why then, begin
To powre first in
Some drops of wine,
In stead of brine,
To search the wound,
So long unsound:
And, when that's done,
Let oyle, next, run,
To cure the sore
Sinne made before.
And O! deare Christ,
E'en as Thou di'st,
Look down, and see
Us weepe for Thee.
And tho, Love knows,
Thy dreadfull woes
Wee cannot ease;
Yet doe Thou please,
Who mercie art,
T'accept each heart,
That gladly would
Helpe, if it could.
Meane while, let mee,
Beneath this tree,
This honour have,
To make my grave.

DEUTERONOMY xxxiii. 25.

As thy days, so shall thy strength be.

Hiereg. 12.

The post
Of swift-foot time
Hath now at length begun
The kalends of our middle stage :
The number'd steps that we have gone, do show
The number of those steps we are to go :
The buds and blossoms of our age
Are blown, decay'd, and gone,
And all our prime
Is lost :
And what we boast too much, we have least cause to
[boast.

Ah me !
There is no rest :
Our time is always fleeing.
What rein can curb our headstrong hours ?
They post away : they pass we know not how :
Our Now is gone, before we can say now :
Time past and future's none of ours :
That hath as yet no being ;
And this hath ceas'd
To be :
What is, is only ours : how short a time have we !

And

Ut Sol ardore virili.

Now like the Sun, He glows with manly Fire :
Invokes the Muse, and strikes the Thracian Lyre.

74 Hungarian rose poem

COMME SI

Une insinuation *simple*

au silence *enroulée avec ironie*

ou

le mystère

précipité

hurlé

dans quelque proche *tourbillon d'hilarité et d'horreur*

voltige *autour du gouffre*

sans le joncher

ni fuir

et en berce le vierge indice

COMME SI

75 French – Stéphane Mallarmé poem

76 French – Guillaume Apollinaire horse calligram

Dagbladen

ZEPPELIN
LONDEN

good bye Piccadilly
SQUARE
farewell Leicester

BEATA INSULA

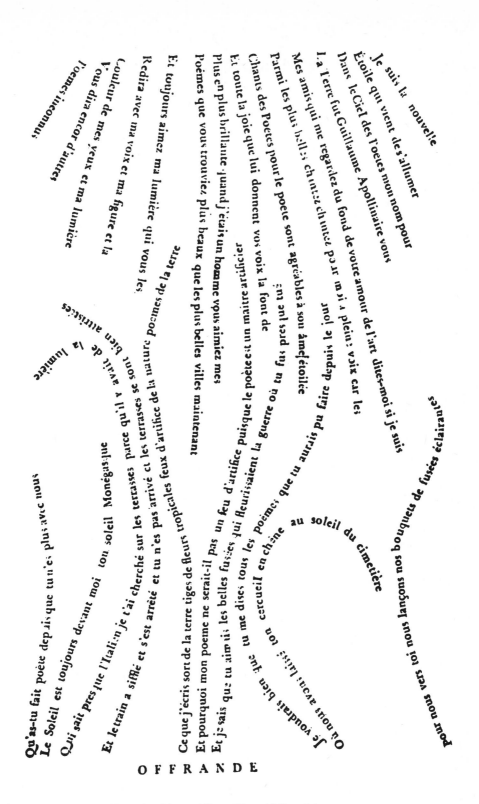

I turn the corner of prayer and burn
In a blessing of the sudden
Sun. In the name of the damned
I would turn back and run
To the hidden land
But the loud sun
Christens down
The sky.
I
Am found.
O let him
Scald me and drown
Me in his world's wound.
His lightning answers my
Cry. My voice burns in his hand.
Now I am lost in the blinding
One. The sun roars at the prayer's end.

I dip this reed
in ink and make
the only way to
live by song in
deed that travels back and forth that rocks
the cradle You anew in dark war's dregs and
in the space so faint who knows what brutal
hand will open an army what eye will fire O
what succubus next what hex and yet do name
Jesus correctly
happy criminals
happy strangers
happy in aliens
with fingertips
printed in fine
grains and blue
in the little O
book of our own
miserichords of
happy mamalujoy
born in the gut
taped bethlehem
hapy hapy lungs

silencio silencio silencio
silencio silencio silencio
silencio   silencio
silencio silencio silencio
silencio silencio silencio

82 Bolivian – Eugen Gomringer 'Silencio'

```
        o
  n o v e l o
  o v o                    s o l
o v o                        o
v e                          l e t r a
l                            e
o                  e s t r e l a          t
                   s   r                  e r r e
  s o l e t r a    r                      e r r e
  o   e   r        e                      t e r r e
  l   t   e        l            t e m o r     o
      r   l        a                      o   t   t
      a   a                t           e   m o r t e
                           t           e       r
          t e r r e m o t o            o   r   m e t r o
                           o           r   t   o
                           r       t e r m o         m   m
                                       e       m o t o r
                                       t       m o t o r
                                       r           t o r t o
                                       o       m o r t o
                                               r   o
```

83 Brazilian – Augusto de Campos 'Terremoto'

n
ni
nic
nich
nicht
nicht
nicht n
nicht nu
nicht nur
nicht nur
nicht nur
nicht nur
nicht nur
nicht nur
nicht nur
nicht nur
nicht nur
nicht nur
nicht nur
nicht nur

informieren   provozieren
informiere   provozieren
informier   provozieren
informie   provozieren
informi   provozieren
inform   provozieren
infor   provozieren
info   provozieren
inf   provozieren
in   provozieren
i   provozieren
               provozieren
               rovozieren
               ovozieren
haltungen   vozieren
altungen   ozieren
ltungen   zieren
tungen   ieren
ungen   eren
ngen   ren
gen   en
en   n
n

laugh laugh
s lover lover s
a si evol love is a
bit a si evol love is a bit
ttib a si evol love is a bitter
tsim rettib a si evol love is a bitter mist
yretsym rettib a si evol love is a bitter mystery
yretsym rettib a si evol love is a bitter mystery
tsim rettib a si evol love is a bitter mist
rettib a si evol love is a bitter
tid a si evol love is a bit
a si evol love is a
s revol lover s
hgual laugh

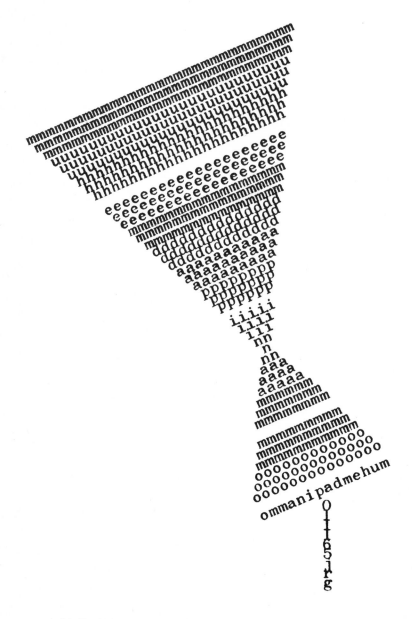

86 English – Robin Greer 'Om Mani Pad Me Hum', Buddhist mantra

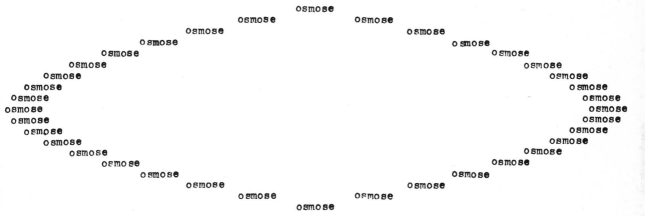

87 French – Ilse and Pierre Garnier 'Osmose Cosmos'

door

obscurity

sound

```
papa dada nana baba caca vava
    papa dada nana baba caca vava
        vava caca baba nana dada papa
            caca baba nana dada papa vava
                nana baba caca vava papa dada
                    dada papa vava caca baba nana
                    dada
                    papa
                    vava
                    caca
                    baba
                    nana
                    nana                                    D
                    baba
A                   caca                                    A
                    vava
P                   papa                                    D
A                   dada
P                   gaga                                    A
A                   gaga
                    gaga
                    gaga
                    dada
                    dada
                    gaga
                    gaga
                    gaga
                    dada papa vava caca baba nana
                nana baba caca vava papa dada
            caca baba nana dada papa vava
        vava caca baba nana dada papa
    papa dada nana baba caca vava
papa dada nana baba caca vava


                                              dada

hommage à dada par hache see, dit chopin      dada
```

89 French – Henri Chopin 'Homage to Dada'

```
rrrrrrrrrrrrrrrrrrrrrrrrrrrrrrrrrrrrrrrrrrrrrrrrrrrrrrr
rrrrrrrrrrrrrrrrrrrrrrrrrrrrrrrrrrrrrrrrrrrrrrrrrrrr   rr
rr                                                      rr
rreeeeeeeeeeeeeeeeeeeeeeeeeeeeeeeeeeeeeeeeeeeeeeeee   rr
rreeeeeeeeeeeeeeeeeeeeeeeeeeeeeeeeeeeeeeeeeeeeeeeeee  ee rr
rree                                              ee rr
rree ttttttttttttttttttttttttttttttttttttttttttttt ee rr
rree tt                                          t ee rr
rree tt aaaaaaaaaaaaaaaaaaaaaaaaaaaaaaaaaaaaaaaaa t ee rr
rree tt aaaaaaaaaaaaaaaaaaaaaaaaaaaaaaaaaaaaaaaaat t ee rr
rree tt aa wwwwwwwwwwwwwwwwwwwwwwwwwwwwwww aa t ee rr
rree tt aa wwwwwwwwwwwwwwwwwwwwwwwwwwwwwww ww aa t ee rr
rree tt aa ww wwww                       ww aa t ee rr
rree tt aa wwccccccccccccccccccccccccccc cc ww aa t ee rr
rree tt aa wwcccccccccccccccccccccccccccc cc ww aa t ee rr
rree tt aa wwcc                          cc ww aa t ee rr
rree tt aa wwcc iiiiiiiiiiiiiiiiiiiiiii   cc ww aa t ee rr
rree tt aa wwcc llliiiiiiiiiiiiiiiiiiiiil cc ww aa t ee rr
rree tt aa wwcc ll                     ll cc ww aa t ee rr
rree tt aa wwcc ll nnnnnnnnnnnnnnnnnll ll cc ww aa t ee rr
rree tt aa wwcc ll nnnnnnnnnnnnnnnnnnll cc ww aa t ee rr
rree tt aa wwcc ll nn 000000000 nnll cc ww aa t ee rr
rree tt aa wwcc ll nn oo      oo nnll cc ww aa t ee rr
rree tt aa wwcc ll nn oossss oo nnll cc ww aa t ee rr
rree tt aa wwcc ll nn oossss oo nnll cc ww aa t ee rr
rree tt aa wwcc ll nn oossss oo nnll cc ww aa t ee rr
rree tt aa wwcc ll nn oo      oo nnll cc ww aa t ee rr
rree tt aa wwcc ll nn 000000000 nnll cc ww aa t ee rr
rree tt aa wwcc ll nn          nnll cc ww aa t ee rr
rree tt aa wwcc ll nnnnnnnnnnnnnnnnnll cc ww aa t ee rr
rree tt aa wwcc ll nnnnnnnnnnnnnnnnnll cc ww aa t ee rr
rree tt aa wwcc lliiiiiiiiiiiiiiiiiii ll cc ww aa t ee rr
rree tt aa wwcc llllllllllllllllllllll cc ww aa t ee rr
rree tt aa wwcccccccccccccccccccccccccc ww aa t ee rr
rree tt aa wwccccccccccccccccccccccccccc ww aa t ee rr
rree tt aa ww                           ww aa t ee rr
rree tt aa wwwwwwwwwwwwwwwwwwwwwwwwwwwwww aa t ee rr
rree tt aa wwwwwwwwwwwwwwwwwwwwwwwwwwwww aa t ee rr
rree tt aa                               aa t ee rr
rree tt aaaaaaaaaaaaaaaaaaaaaaaaaaaaaaaaaaaaaaa t ee rr
rree tt aaaaaaaaaaaaaaaaaaaaaaaaaaaaaaaaaaaaaat t ee rr
rree tt                                          t ee rr
rree ttttttttttttttttttttttttttttttttttttttttttttt ee rr
rree                                              ee rr
rreeeeeeeeeeeeeeeeeeeeeeeeeeeeeeeeeeeeeeeeeeeeeeeee  ee rr
rreeeeeeeeeeeeeeeeeeeeeeeeeeeeeeeeeeeeeeeeeeeeeeeee   rr
rr                                                      rr
rrrrrrrrrrrrrrrrrrrrrrrrrrrrrrrrrrrrrrrrrrrrrrrrrrrr   rr
rrrrrrrrrrrrrrrrrrrrrrrrrrrrrrrrrrrrrrrrrrrrrrrrrrrrrrr
```

91 English – John Furnival 'Tours de Babel Changées en Ponts'

spazio spazio spazio spazio spazio spazio spazio spazio spazio spazio spazio
spazio spazio spazio spazio spazio spazio spazio spazio spazio spazio spazio
spazio spazio spazio spazio spazio spazio spazio spazio spazio spazio spazio
spazio spazio spazio spazio spazio spazio spazio spazio spazio spazio spazio
spazio spazio spazio spazio spazio spazio spazio spazio spazio spazio spazio
spazio spazio spazio spazio spazio spazio spazio spazio spazio spazio spazio
spazio spazio spazio spazio spazio spazio spazio spazio spazio spazio spazio
spazio spazio spazio spazio spazio spazio spazio spazio spazio spazio spazio
spazio spazio spazio spazio spazio spazio spazio spazio spazio spazio spazio spazio spazio spazio
spazio spazio spazi spazio spazio spazio spazio spazio spazio spazio spazio spazio spazio spazio spazio spazio pazio spazio spazio
spazio spazio spazi spazio spazio spazio spazio spazio spazio spazio spazio spazio spazio spazio spazio pazio spazio spazio
spazio spazio spazi spazio spazio spazio spazio spazio spazio spazio spazio spazio spazio spazio spazio pazio spazio spazio
spazio spazio spazi spazio spazio spazio spazio spazio spazio spazio spazio spazio spazio spazio spazio pazio spazio spazio
spazio spazio spazi spazio spazio spazio spazio spazio spazio spazio spazio spazio spazio spazio spazio pazio spazio spazio
spazio spazio spazi spazio spazio spazio spazio spazio spazio spazio spazio spazio spazio pazio spazio spazio
spazio spazio spazi spazio spazio spazio spazio spazio spazio spazio spazio spazio spazio pazio spazio spazio
spazio spazio spazi spazio spazio spazi spazio spazio spazio spazio spazio spazio spazio spazio pazio spazio spazio
spazio spazio spazi spazio spazio spazi spazio spazio spazio spazio spazio spazio spazio pazio spazio spazio
spazio spazio spazi spazio spazio spaz spazio spazio spazio spazio spazio spazio spazio pazio spazio spazio
spazio spazio spazi spazio spazio spaz spazio spazio spazio spazio spazio spazio spazio pazio spazio spazio
spazio spazio spazi spazio spazio spaz spazio spazio spazio spazio spazio spazio spazio pazio spazio spazio
spazio spazio spazi spazio spazio spaz spazio spazio spazio spazio spazio spazio spazio pazio spazio spazio
spazio spazio spazi spazio spazio spaz spazio spazio spazio spazio spazio spazio spazio pazio spazio spazio
spazio spazio spazi spazio spazio spaz spazio spazio spazio spazio spazio spazio spazio pazio spazio spazio
spazio spazio spazi spazio spazio spaz spazio spazio spazio spazio spazio spazio pazio spazio spazio
spazio spazio spazi spazio spazio spazio spazio spazio spazio spazio spazio spazio spazio spazio pazio spazio spazio
spazio spazio spazi spazio spazio spazio spazio spazio spazio spazio spazio spazio spazio spazio pazio spazio spazio
spazio spazio spazi spazio spazio spazio spazio spazio spazio spazio spazio spazio spazio spazio pazio spazio spazio
spazio spazio spazi spazio spazio spazio spazio spazio spazio spazio spazio spazio spazio spazio pazio spazio spazio
spazio spazio spazio spazio spazio spazio spazio spazio spazio spazio spazio spazio spazio spazio spazio spazio
spazio spazio spazio spazio spazio spazio spazio spazio spazio spazio spazio
spazio spazio spazio spazio spazio spazio spazio spazio spazio spazio spazio
spazio spazio spazio spazio spazio spazio spazio spazio spazio spazio spazio
spazio spazio spazio spazio spazio spazio spazio spazio spazio spazio spazio
spazio spazio spazio spazio spazio spazio spazio spazio spazio spazio spazio
spazio spazio spazio spazio spazio spazio spazio spazio spazio spazio spazio
spazio spazio spazio spazio spazio spazio spazio spazio spazio spazio spazio

92 Italian – Arrigo Lora Totino 'Spazio'

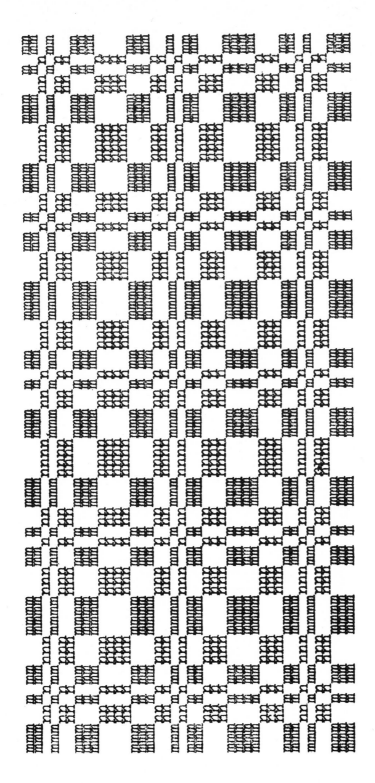

93 English – Charles Cameron 'Poem for Rosemarie'

94 Russian – Valerian Neretchnikov, tree from random letters

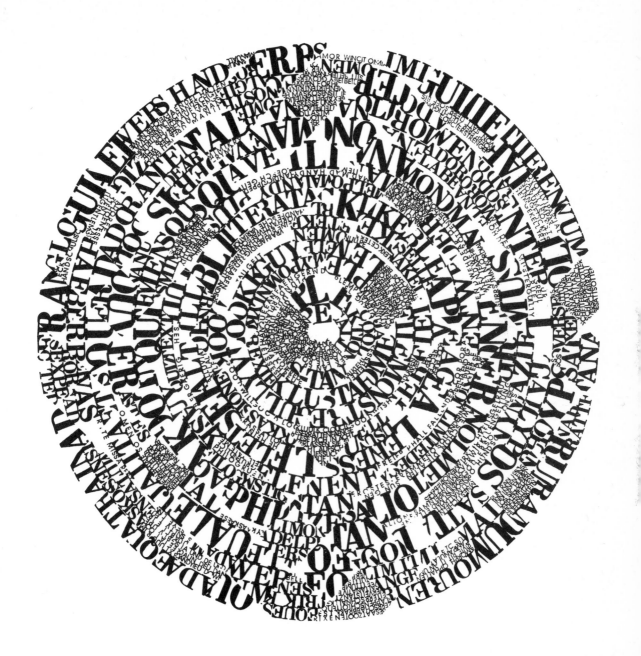

95 German – Ferdinand Kriwet poster

96 German – Carlfriedrich Claus 'Allegorical Essay for Albert Wigand'

97 American – Carl Fernbach-Flarsheim 'Mirror Field inside Random Field'

98 German – Franz Mon 'Stuttgart'

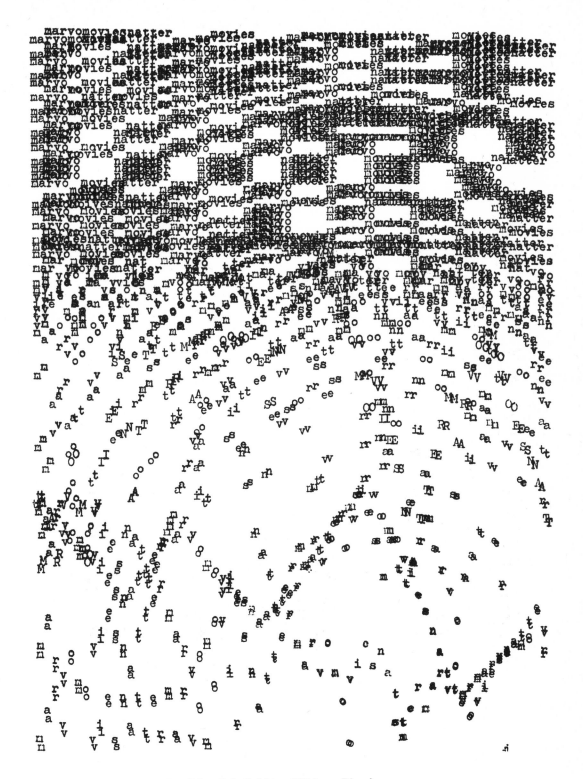

99 English – Bob Cobbing 'Whisper Piece'

100 Austrian – Heinz Gappmeyr 'Zeichen'

101 England – grave stone at Godstone

Notes to illustrations

[1] 'Poems in the Shapes of Things', *Art News Annual*, 1959.

ENDPAPER LEFT
Aramaic. Incantation bowl. Syriac script. The angel Gabriel and various idols and spirits are invoked to protect Chozroes, son of Aprahormiz, and his family. 6th century AD.
British Museum, London

ENDPAPER RIGHT
Aramaic. Incantation bowl inscribed with magical incantation in Babylonian Aramaic, written in square Hebrew characters in the form of a get or divorce writ pronounced against Lilith and the devils who plague a woman, Nowandich, and her family. Nippur, Iraq. 6th century AD.
British Museum, London

1   Egyptian. Inner coffin of Besenmut, a priest of Aman-Re. The mummy case is covered with inscriptions from *The Book of the Dead*, a collection of maxims for the guidance of the soul after death – a book equal in spiritual thought to the later Hebrew scriptures. Possibly from Thebes. XXII Dynasty, 900 BC
British Museum, London

2   Chinese. Folk amulet against asthma. The amulet is to be burnt and the ashes drunk with wine. The diseased will expect a fever and then be healed. These Taoist amulets were collected early in the 19th century from street corners and temples. They are currently sold at the temples of Tao-che or by Buddhist priests (bonzes) for money or rice. The shapes are anthropomorphic with odd discernible words cast in, with magical formulae impossible to comprehend and characters which are entirely invented. They are usually written on yellow paper in vermilion script, since yellow is considered by the Chinese to be the colour of the earth and of the legendary emperor Huang-Ti, the Yellow Emperor – one of the sages who transmitted a belief in magic. These talismans are undatable, since they are part of a long folk tradition. From Père François Sebastian Doré *Recherches sur les Superstitions en Chine* 18v. Shanghai 1911-38

3   Chinese. Talisman against ghosts designed by the bonzes to be worn on the shield, assuring the warrior that he would never again be troubled by ghosts.
Père Doré *op. cit.*

4   Chinese. Buddhist magic formula for curing pain in the side. It is glued over the lungs or on the place where pain is most severe.
Père Doré *op. cit.*

5   Chinese. Buddhist rosary prayer. Recited for happiness in the next world and for attaining merit to arrive there. Used by vegetarians. 18th century.
Père Doré *op. cit.*

6 Chinese. Taoist exhortation against the killing and eating of oxen. Reading from the neck to the tail are the words: 'First do not wait for the time that will never come. That time is called regret and it is always too late. It is wrong to kill any thing that is alive.' The text goes on to describe reasons against killing and the punishments in store for the wrongdoer.
Père Doré *op. cit.*

7a Chinese. Stone rubbing. K'ui Hsing, the god of literature, made of the characters of his name. The calligraphy is by Ma-Te-Chao. Located in Loyang, China. Undated.
Peter Mayer, London

The Chinese estimation of calligraphy is that it may be technically able or skilful. But this is faint praise. In the category above this it may be wonderful. 'But the brush strokes of the divine calligraphers are divine and divine in the specific sense that they penetrate the highest being.' (O. Sirén *The Chinese on the Art of Painting* Peiping 1936.)

7b Chinese. Stone rubbing. The god of longevity made from the text 'The way permeates heaven and earth. Its qualities transcend its form.' Text by Yuan Shen, calligraphy by Tung Tse-San. Loyang, China. Undated.
Peter Mayer, London

8a Japanese. Zen calligraphy by Sekijo Yeseiji Hakuin (1685-1708). The highly abstract characters read 'The sterile woman gives birth in the night.'
Hosokawa Collection, Tokyo.

This piece of Zen calligraphy is a demonstration of the precept of Satori – the direct transmission which reveals the divine in oneself and in the universe. The calligraphy itself is a form of meditation and intuition.

8b Japanese. Calligraphic portrait of Tenjin-Sama on his return from China by Hakuin. Sugawara Michizane, eminent scholar and politician (called Tenjin), was exiled from the court at Kyoto during the Uda reign, 887-897. When he died, disasters befell the court. Therefore to propitiate his ghost, he was deified. In this portrait, the hair and clothing are composed of characters.
Aujourd'hui Art and Architecture no 44, January 1964

9 Japanese. Waka poem by Minamoto-no-Shitago, one of the thirty-six poets, arranged in the form of an acrostic, so that the poems interlink with one another and may be read in various directions. A transcription of the acrostic in modern printed form appears above the illustration. It was composed in the later part of the Heian period (12th century). There are 36 tonkas, which are 31 syllable poems, one in each square.
British Museum, London.

10 Japanese. Portrait of Ono-no-Komachi, one of the famous six poets of ancient Japan, by Hokusai. The 31-syllable poem, written in highly figurative grass script (socho), reads, 'A flower that fades with no outward sign is the heart of a man in this world.' The robes of the poet are a calligraphic representation of her name. 19th century
British Museum, London

11 Malayan. Flag of the Sultan of Kalanton, a state in N.E. Malaya. The calligraphic tiger, composed of Arabic letters, reads, 'Government of Kalanton. The help of God and victory are near. Spread this good news to the believers.' (Koran 61:13) These words are well known and are often used to convey the victory of Islam over its enemies. The lion is the Symbol of Ali, but it is frequently interchanged with the tiger. It has been suggested that the two beasts might be merged in the folk mind.
C. Hooytas 'Flags of the Malay Peninsula' *Journal of the Straits Branch of the Royal Asiatic Society* April 1917

12 Burmese. Lotus bud writing from a literary miscellany of archaic Burmese poems called *Parana Depani Kyam I*, by Maw-bi Saya Thein, Rangoon, 1930. The poem is written in an extremely complex style, with the outside line read after the rest, and a repeated centre line. It is a love poem by a young girl lamenting the loss of her beloved who has left on a mission of war. Possibly 18th century.

13 Burmese. Seven wheel jewel writing. The centre word is read as belonging to every line. It is a glorification of the king's power – the universal monarch – the super-mondial being. The seven petals of the lotus flower figures in Burmese mysticism, and the open lotus bloom is often used symbolically for the deity, not only in Burma but in Tantric Buddhism, Animism and Hinduism.
Maw-bi Saya Thein *op. cit*.

14 Tibetan. Scorpion charm, a guard against all injuries from malignant demons dangerous to women, red demons and earth demons. The figures are hemmed in by the mystic syllables 'Jsa! Hūm! Hūm! Bam! Ho!' Every orthodox monastery in Tibet keeps a sorcerer. 1 *Naga*, snake spirit; 2 *Tsan*, devil; 3 *Ma-mo*, fiendess; 4 King-fiend.
L. A. Waddell *Lamaism* Cambridge 1939.

15 Tibetan. The Tutelary Tam-din's charm. The Tam-din is the favourite Lamaist demon. Each Lamaist sect has its own special tutelary fiend who accompanies the sect and guards their footsteps from mirror fiends. The Lama utters certain mantras and coerces the demon king into investing the

Lama's person with his awful demonic aspect. The Lama then is free to walk out, safe from demons, who take him to be their own demon king.
L. A. Waddell *op. cit.*

16 Tibetan. Yantra of Manjusri, a symbolic diagram conceived in meditation and used for spiritual development in Tibetan Buddhism. The yantra is a geometrical design of mystical significance, made to establish telepathic communication with the deity. In art, yantras are projected as mandalas or magic circles. According to mystical theory these words should be sung, chanted, spoken, murmured, mumbled or whispered, or gazed at intently. The God, Om, resides in the innermost part. 19th century.
L. A. Waddell *op. cit.*

17 Tibetan. A mystic monogram entitled The All-Powerful Ten. For the mystic, the name of a thing is as real as the thing itself. This monogram, like the Om – the mystic name of the deity, signifying creator, preserver, destroyer – is to be contemplated in order to reach a state of enlightenment.
L. A. Waddell *op. cit.*

18 Urdu. Lion (tiger), see note 11. Moslem amulet figuring Ali's tomb at Najaf in the background. The inscription above the animal reads, 'This is an amulet to be hung on the wall of a home that has been properly cleaned. And that whoever he be, Christian, Hindu or Moslem, he shall be spared the company of evil spirits if he but believe in this charm. These words have been written in a holy time and a holy place.' The figure itself contains upside down and in mirror image the word 'Ali'; the neck, in mirror image, 'Muhammad the pure'; the body, in mirror image, 'Every soul becomes clear . . . through your saintliness and devotion'. This amulet might well be sold at the shrine of Ali, even today. 19th century.
Victoria and Albert Museum, London

19 Indian. Symbol for Om – the highest name of God. It is sometimes explained as a representation of the individual and the divine consciousness, which are in essence identical. The lower, longer curve represents the waking state; the upper curve the state of dreamless sleep. The curve springing from the junction of these two represents the dreaming condition. The semi-circle and dot represent the state of liberation which is beyond the other three states. The incomplete circle represents infinity. It can also be seen as the sun and moon, and as the copulation of Shiva and Kali during which it is said the sacred syllable 'Om' was uttered.
Hari Prasad Sohastri *The Practice of Yoga* London 1957

20 Bengali. Mangal Kalsh, a holy vase placed in the temple to store holy water from the Ganges or Kalash rivers. The words 'Sri Ram' are repeated over and over again. The calligrapher's name is written at the bottom – Srutilankadasbanikya. 19th century.
Victoria and Albert Museum, London

21 Indian. Mahadeva or Shiva begging rice from Parvati or Annapurna. The two designations of the goddess make up all the figures – Sri Durga and Durga Purna. Shiva is the lord of songs, the creator and the destroyer. He is worshipped as the lingam. Annapurna, both mild and fierce, is the nourisher, worshiped as the yoni. Shiva's bull and Annapurna's lion appear created from her name. She sits on an open lotus blossom. 19th century.
Victoria and Albert Museum, London

22 Sanskrit. Hanuman, the monkey-chief, devotee of lord Rama. When he opened his heart for examination he was seen to be inscribed within with praises of his lord. Sent one day to find a cure on Mount Kaitasa for Rama's sick son, he brought back the entire mountain, which he carries in his right hand. The figure is composed of the story of Hanuman's life from birth to death – the Vayu-Stuti by Trivikramacarya.
19th-century edition of the Ramayana – ancient Indian epic.

23 Urdu. Horse with hunter. The verse in the right-hand corner provides the key to the figure. It reads: Notice this beautiful verse of Bahadur Shah
and hang it in your home.
Oh where are the days gone
when princes strode the earth?
In the crown you will find
the prince's name, his date of birth.
The horse he rides has two verses
and a third verse is here
for those who have the wit
to discover it.
It concerns a hunted beast.
The verses are from the famous 13th-century *Gulistan:*
The Arabian horse though he is slim
is even so worth a herd of asses.
and
The slender-waisted horse proves useful
on the day of battle, not the fatted ox.
The hare reads: Never underestimate the power of your adversary.
Printed 1912.
Victoria and Albert Museum, London

24 Urdu. Elephant. The name and designation of the Nawab of Twara. 'The late, unique in rule and headship, high in rank and title . . . treasurer of the royal (or holy) gracious presence. 19th century.
Victoria and Albert Museum, London

25 Ethiopian. Medical and magical text, from the Awda Nagast (The Circle of Kings). By means of these circles it is claimed that the fate of human beings can be forecast. 18th century.
British Museum, London

26 Ethiopian. As note 25. These Christian texts are apotropaic, designed to ward off evil spirits. They are mainly unreadable, consisting of magical formulae and familiar symbols – the lamb, the three kings, the donkey – as well as the more primitive double snake, and the good as opposed to evil eye.
British Museum, London

27 Moroccan. Travelling amulet. Muhammad's footprint. The text reports a traditional tale of the prophet while he was still living with his wife, Ayesha. The marginal writings suggest mystical and amuletic properties. Modern.
H. T. Norris SOAS London

28 Persian. Bird tughra. Inscribed with the Bismillah 'I commence it in the name of God who is very kind and merciful'. 19th century.
Bibliothèque Nationale, Paris

Tughra writings are the most ingenious use of Arabic script. A sentence from the Koran or a common prayer is written in a way that the composition outlines a bird, tiger, elephant or any other animal that is not considered unclean or of ill omen. These are then used by superstitious masses, protecting the keepers from the malicious influence of evil spirits. These animal figures form a very common object of decoration in Moslem homes, despite the ban put on them by priests and by the Koran itself.

29 Persian. Amuletic tughra' A face consisting of the words 'Allah', upside down, at the top; 'Muhammad', the pupil and cheek; 'Ali', upside down, the nose and eye; 'Hasan', the chin.
M. Ziuddin *Monograph of Moslem calligraphy* Madras 1936

30 Persian. Two horses composing an invocation to Muhammad: 'May God grant peace and blessing to Muhammad as he has already granted to Abraham.'
British Museum, London

31 Arabic. Prayer. Double script – each half of the script mirrors the other. This is a common phenomenon. (See 29 and 30) It reads, 'Say each man is his own example. Your God knows who of you walks most straight on the path of righteousness.' 19th century.
Kamel Al-Baba 'Calligraphy a noble Art' *Aramco World* July-August 1964

32 Arabic. Mosque with four minarets. Kufic script. It reads, 'There is no strength and no power but that of the almighty and all-powerful God.'
Kamel Al-Baba *op. cit.*
The Kufic script is hieratic, therefore the early Korans were written exclusively in this style. It is a beautiful monumental writing which takes its name from the Mesopotamian town of Kufa and its school, where the script was practised by famous calligraphers from the end of the 7th century.

33 Persian Lion, composed of the introductory prayer from the *Gulistan*, by the poet Sa'di, written in 1258. The *Gulistan* is a collection of moral anecdotes and is widely read throughout the Arabic world. The prayer reads, 'Praise be to God, the great and glorious, for his worship is the means of drawing nigh to Him, and in grateful acknowledgment to Him is increase in blessings.' 18th century.
British Museum, London

34 Turkish. Dervish wall hanging. The word Ali is made by the representation of the zulfikar or sword that forms the centrepiece. Here the family of Muhammad is represented. Ali was adopted by Muhammad. He married Fatima and had two sons, Hasan and Huseyin. The Dervishes are an unorthodox sect which uses these representations for mystical and magical purposes.
T. K. Birge *The Bektashi Order of Dervishes* London 1952

35 Turkish. Dervish lion, which serves to express to the initiated and to conceal from the outsider, and especially the orthodox Sunni, the essential doctrine of Ali's significance. It reads , 'Ali is the lion of God, the attribute of the merciful. Verily, Ali is my lord.' 19th century.
T. K. Birge *op. cit.*

36 Turkish. Dervish wall hanging. The lion and the tiger appear to be interchangeable for the Moslems, both signifying the strength of Ali. This tiger reads, in part, 'In the name of the lion of God, the face of God, the victorious Ali, the son of Ebu Talet.' 19th century.
T. K. Birge *op. cit.*

37 Turkish. Oilcloth chart. 'O Ali' is written in large letters and reversed, with Muhammad and Allah written in smaller letters, all composed of finer inscriptions in the larger letters. The 'O Ali' contains Koran 17, and the Allah is formed from Koran 24:35, known as 'the glorification of the candle'. The word Muhammad is made by the arrangement of Koran 48:29. Across the top is a sentence from Koran 42:22, 'Say further I ask no reward of you save the love of my kin.' In the middle, at the top, 'Glorious is his divine Majesty.' Hasan and Huseyin is written in black letters and underneath Muhammad is the name of Fatima Uzzehra. These five are sometimes represented by a hand with its five fingers open. 1908.   T. K. Birge *op. cit.*

38 Turkish. Mosque in double script writing. It reads, 'He is all powerful.' Malik Aksel 'Das Schrift-Bild in der Turkischen Kunst' *Antolica* no 1 1967

39 Turkish. Man. God or Allah composes the head; Muhammad, the prophet, the sides; Ali, the cousin and son-in-law of Muhammad, and the fourth caliph, is in the chest; Hasan and Huseyin, the sons of Fatima and Ali, the outsides.   Malik Aksel *op. cit.*

40 Turkish. Figure of a zodiacal man. Across the top is written, 'And the most high said: In the name of God the merciful, the compassionate, we will show them signs in different countries and among themselves, until it becomes plain to them that it is the truth.' (Koran 41:53) In the right-hand medallion, 'Now come O ye seeker for the divine love. There is no doubt but that the holy body of the gnostic in God and of the perfect man is the most great copy. First of all are the seven layers. The layers of earth compare to those of heaven. The veins are the rivers; the bone marrow the mines; the large hairs the trees; the small hairs the plants; his sadness the clouds; his tears are the rain; his sweat is the dew; his holy speech is the phoenix; his good deeds are the angels; his vain deeds are the animals. God most high has repeated and taught to Adam all the names. Even the verse and chapter which we have created, the symbol of them is in man.' In the left-hand medallion are the words, 'The nature of man is various. His evil nature is the ferocious animal; his carnal nature is Satan; his youth the spring; his vigorous manhood midsummer; his old age autumn; his worry and anxiety are reproach, punishment and suffering like winter. His carnal instinct the anti-Christ; his saintly spirit is Jesus; his sickness is the sign of the end of the world; his mouth is the door of repentance; his sleep is death; his waking the resurrection.' The writing formed on the figure reflects the idea that the body of man represents the entire order of the universe, the movement of the spheres, the seasons, the varieties of nature. And in his body are to be found the zodiacal signs. The word Ali is written in his moustache. Undated, ancient.   T. K. Birge *op. cit.*

41 Turkish. Circle ode or ghazal by Shahin Ghiray – Khan of the Crimea during Catherine the Great's reign. A long love poem beginning, 'Let but my beloved come and take up her abode in the mansion of her love and shall not thy beautiful face cause his eyes to sparkle with delight . . . If thou art wise, erect an inn on the road of self-negation, so that the pilgrims of holy love can make there their halting place.' The poem continues at length and ends, 'It is true that lovers do unremittingly dedicate their talents to the praise of their mistress; but has thy turn yet come, O Shahin Ghiray, so to offer thy tribute of libation?' *c.* 1768.
J. W. Redhouse 'The Turkish Circle Ode' *Journal of the Royal Asiatic Society* vol. 18 1861

42 Armenian. Talismanic frontispiece to a medical, magical textbook. This page is meant to be tied to a part of the body for healing purposes. It invokes the healing power of two saints, and a martyr who was an unpaid doctor. Antioch. 18th century.
Artin Hazarian, New York

43 Armenian. Prayer for mercy, concluding, 'You are the way, the truth, and the life. Do not neglect me, your servant, that I might die in sin. Have mercy for the sake of all the passion you endured with great patience. Make the evil princes of the dark, who struggle with your servant, perish invisibly.' This manuscript in the form of a parchment scroll was written by the scribe Mgerdich at Nakitchervari near Etchmiadzin in 1703.
Artin Hazarian, New York

44a Hebrew. Amulets for childbirth from the *Sefer Raziel*, an amulet maker's
& b handbook by Rabbi Eleazor of Worms (1176-1238). Two triangles are placed in a circle. In one the triangles are intertwined to form a hexagram; in the other they are placed base to base. The text (Exodus 11:8), in the form of diminishing lozenges, appears in both.
T. Schrire *Hebrew Amulets* London 1966

45 Hebrew. King, from the Mathzav or festival prayers for the New Year, according to the Italian rite. The prayer ends with the words: 'Keep us from plagues, swords, starvation, captivity, poverty, destruction, epidemics. And write down a life of goodness for the children of your faith. And all creation will thank you . . . You of good name.' 13th or 14th century.
British Museum, London

46 Hebrew. Page from an illuminated manuscript containing the Massorah Parva. 1491.
British Museum, London

In some Hebrew manuscripts the massorah, which is the critical emendation found on certain pages of the Bible, ceases to be the usual three lines, in minuscule letters, surrounding the biblical text. Unexpectedly, in some manuscripts the massorah is shaped into patterns which generally have no particular relevance to the biblical passage, or to the emendations and alternative readings which are the stuff of the critical commentary. The strange intrusions can appear either as a full page decoration, as in this illustration, or in corners of the page. There is no apparent reason for their appearance. Some manuscripts are full of these designs, some have an occasional one, and most have none, merely the conventional three-line critical marginalia that have accompanied massoretic bibles since the Talmudic age. (See also Berjouhi Bowler 'The Word as Ikon' *Typographica* no 8 London 1968)

47 Hebrew. Massoretic text, as above, Pentateuch. Early 14th century. *British Museum, London*

48 Hebrew. Massoretic text, as above, German bible, Pentateuch. 14th century. *Kongelige Bibliotek, Copenhagen*

49 Hebrew. Massoretic text, as above, German bible, Pentateuch, minuscule lettering form a minorah, 1298. *Bibliothèque Nationale, Paris*

50 Hebrew. Massoretic text, as above, German bible, Pentateuch. Reproduction greatly enlarged. 14th century. *British Museum, London*

51 Hebrew. Massoretic text, as above, from a manuscript containing the Pentateuch with the Torqum, the massorah, Haptaroth, the five megilloth and the Book of Job. This depicts Jonah beneath the gourd. 14th century. *British Museum, London*

52 Hebrew. Massoretic text, as above, from same manuscript as 51. Jonah and the whale. 14th century. *British Museum, London*

53 Hebrew. Massoretic text, as above. Greatly enlarged decoration from the Pentateuch. 14th century. *British Museum, London*

54 Greek. Magical papyrus; diminishing lozenges; an amulet placed in the mouth of a corpse. Its purpose is to force the spirit of the dead to bring the

desired woman into the possession of the entreator. 'So long as this charm rests in the mouth, the lady-love Karosa will come burning with passion into the arms of the magician Apolos.' 5th century BC.
Carl Preisandanz *Papyri Graecae Magicae* Berlin 1928

55 Greek. Magical papyrus; the decapitated god, a figure containing mystic vowels. It contains a magic text to be copied and worn as an amulet. The earth is said to have sprung from the blood spouting from the neck of the headless god. The seven gnostic vowels stand for the seven planets, the seven notes of the musical scale, as well as many other cosmic references apparent to the initiated. 5th century BC.
Carl Preisandanz *op. cit. ibid.*

56 Greek. Cross from an Evangelestarium – lessons for the service of the Greek Orthodox Church, using passages from the Bible. This page is from John 6: 40-51, concerning the transubstantiation. Each page of this rare manuscript is shaped as a cross. It was brought out on feast days to show the populace, together with saints' relics, at the monastery of Pantocratorus on Mt Athos. Written by Emperor Alexus Commeus, 970.
British Museum, London.

57 Greek. Egg by Simias. The technique of reading this poem is described in the Introduction. It is a bucolic poem, using the shape as a metaphor for the poetic process. The opening lines read, 'Behold here a new foundling of a twittering mother, a Dorian nightingale. Receive it well since the mother was pure and laboured shrilly for it.' Rhodes, 300 BC.
Charles Bottenhouse 'Poems in the Shapes of Things' *Art News Annual* no 28 1959

58 Greek. Altar by Besantinus. The altar calligram is a recurring favourite, appearing in anthologies from 300 BC to the 18th century. This poem, like the Simias egg, uses its metaphorical shape as a realization of the nature of poetry. Unlike the real altar, which must sustain sacrificial bloodstains and smoke from burnt offerings, the altar of Besantinus has been reared by the Muses 'to whose art the King of the Gods granted immortality'. Rome, AD 100.
Charles Boltenhouse *op. cit.*

59 Latin. 'Carmina Figurata', by Porfyrius Optatianus. Porfyrius is the earliest known poet to have composed this type of figured poem which was later to be developed extensively in Carolingian times by poets such as Alcuin and Boniface. The poems of Porfyrius are usually dedicated to Constantine as a panegyric. The virtuosity of the work rests in its complex acrostic nature.

Certain phrases appear and reappear to be read across, down, up, as well as diagonally. The patterned areas can be read separately, and as part of the poem written as a square in hexameters. There are vague references to piety and sanctity and invocations of the Greek Muses. In this manuscript the Greek sign for Christ – chi rho – appears as a mast of a ship with oars. Byzantium, AD 325.
Jahrbuch der Kunsthistorischen Sammlungen des Auerhochsten Kaiserhauses XIII 1892

60   Latin. 'Carmina Figurata', by Porfyrius Optatianus. This is a 20th-century setting of the same poem as in illustration 59.
Elsa Kluge *Optatianus, Porfyrius Publius, 'Carmine Figurata'* 1926.

It is curious that the word Carmine originally meant spell or charm before it came to mean song.

61   Latin. 'Christ on the Cross', by St Hrabanus Maurus, Carolingian poet and theologian from Germany, b. 786. The figure, which overlays the pious poem, also contains a verse to be read separately as well as part of the larger area. For example, the hair of Christ includes the words 'Lord of Justice'. These letters can be read across as well as pulled out of the drawn area. The loin-cloth of Christ contains the words 'He who wears this small cloth contains the entire universe in his hands, the stars and the earth.'
National Bibliothek, Vienna

62   Latin. 'The Lamb of God and the Four Apocalyptic Symbols', by St Hrabanus Maurus. In the Revelations the beasts are described: 'And the first beast was like a lion and the second was like a calf and the third beast had the face of a man and the fourth beast was like a flying eagle.' Here each animal figures in a separate text with special references to their qualities. In the lamb are the words, 'Behold the Lamb of God who removes the sins of the world.' This poem itself begins as a prayer, 'Son of the Supreme Father, grant me . . .' 8th century.
National Bibliothek, Vienna

63   Latin. *Phaenomena*, by Aratus of Soli (b. 260 BC), translated by Cicero, and here rendered by a Carolingian scribe in the 9th or 10th century AD. Aratus in this poem gives an astronomical description of the heavens according to the system of Eudoxus, the astronomer, introducing the fabulous history attached to the constellations from pagan mythology. Without a hero, events or dialogue, nevertheless it was held to be the most popular poem in the classical world for 5 or 6 centuries. It was estimated the equal of Homer's *Iliad*. There were many Roman translations of the original Greek text. The one copied in these illustrations is Cicero's. The poem was even quoted by St Paul as proof that the doctrine of eternity, unity and omnipotence of the

Godhead was not a new invention nor merely confined to the Jews. Thus it became an extremely popular poem for the early Christians. The *Phaenomena* is divided into three parts – a description of the constellations, the position of the most important circles on the celestial sphere, and the position of various other constellations on the rising of each of the signs of the zodiac.
This illustration shows Jove, the Sun, Mars, Venus and Mercury.
British Museum, London

64 Latin. *Phaenomena*, as above. Perseus, a naked winged warrior, bearing in his right hand a drawn sword and in his left hand the head of Medusa. The scribe has drawn the figure to contain the verse about this constellation.
British Museum, London

65 Latin. *Phaenomena*, as above. Cygnus, or the Swan, with expanded wings and outstretched neck. This is the adulterous bird who brought about the betrayal of Leda.
British Museum, London

66 Latin. *Phaenomena*, as above. Argo, the ship which carried Jason on his search for the Golden Fleece.
British Museum, London

67 Latin. From a manuscript containing ecclesiastical computations and including part of Cicero's translation of the Aratus (see above). Here again is the *Phaenomena*, figured by a different scribe in AD 1107. This page concerns Sagitta, the arrow or dart.
British Museum, London

68 Latin. As above. Orion, the giant hunter, who wears belt and sword and carries a club. The constellation was of great importance to the early astronomers.

69 German. Gothic calligram containing Luke 1: 68-79: 'Blessed be the Lord God of Israel for he hath visited and redeemed his people.' The scribe is Wolfgang Fuggen.
Nutzlich und Wolgegrundt Formular Manncherlen Schöner Schrieften Mnich Munich 1553

70 English. A cut-out in the form of a sceptre and orb with a cross, containing the Ten Commandments floriated round the hand of God.
R. Jackman *Manuscript Examples* London 1620

71 Latin. Emblem in the form of a tree, entitled 'Boni Principis Encomium' (The praise of a good prince). The sentence on which the lines turn is 'Elisabetham Reginam Diu nobis servet Iesus incolumen. Amen.' (Long may Jesus keep Queen Elizabeth safe for us.)
Andrew Willett *Sacrorum Emblemata Centuria Una* Cambridge 1596.

72 English. Robert Herrick 'The Cross' London 1647. Many metaphysical poets used the figure poem for their religious texts.

73 English. Francis Quarles *Hieroglyphics* London 1658

74 Hungarian. Rose poem. The text, written in Latin, proceeds from the outer petals to the inner, and celebrates spring and flowers. It is a literalization of the flower love poem tradition in the Hungarian baroque. The name Ioannes Caspar appears on the outer petals. Collected by Lepsenyi István in the manuscript 'Poesis Ludens seu artificia poetica, quaedam ex variis Authoribus collecta', 1700.   *National Szechenyi Library, Budapest*

75 French. From 'Un Coup De Dés Jamais N'Abolira Le Hasard, Poème' (A dice throw will never abolish chance, a poem) by Stéphane Mallarmé, 1897. Reading across the page, the lines read, 'As if / a simple insinuation wreathed around with irony / or the mystery cast down howled in some nearby vortex of hilarity and horror / hovers around the gulf without strewing it or fleeing / and cradles its virgin index / as if (See Introduction).

In the *Pilot Plan for Concrete Poetry*, written by the Brazilian Noigandres group in 1958, Mallarmé is hailed as a forerunner of their work, having made the first qualitative jump, 'subdivisions prismatiques de l'idée'; space (blanks) and typographical devices as substantive elements of composition.

76 French. 'Tout Terriblement', a horse calligram by Guillaume Apollinaire. The opening lines read, 'You will find here a new representation of the universe. The most poetic and the most modern.'
Guillaume Apollinaire *Calligrammes* 1918

Like Mallarmé, Apollinaire is mentioned in the *Pilot Plan for Concrete Poetry* for his method of composition based on 'direct-analogical not logical-discursive juxtaposition of elements'; for his regard for synthesis rather than analysis.

77 Italian. Poem in the form of a letter from a soldier to his sweetheart describing his experiences in the war.
Filippo Tommaso Marinetti *Les Mots en Liberté Futuristes*

The Futurists, led by Marinetti, were committed to the destruction of syntax, to the liberated word and imagination without bounds. Poetry must be a violent onslaught. There is no masterpiece without aggression. Marinetti's original use of typography has not been superseded. His use of letters to produce sound qualities has been seminal to the opto-phonetic poems of Hausman and Schwitters, and to the concretists such as Ernst Jandl and Bob Cobbing.

78 Flemish. 'Zeppelin'.
Paul Van Ostaijen *Bezette Stad* (Occupied City) Antwerp 1921.

79 French. 'Offrande', an Homage to Guillaume Apollinaire.
Pierre Albert-Birot 1921

80 English. 'Axe shape.' Dylan Thomas *Vision and Prayer* 1946

81 American. Cross shape by Jack Hirschman 1968.

82 Bolivian. 'Silencio' 1954. Eugen Gomringer *The Constellations* 1963

The texts which follow belong to the International Concrete Poetry Movement, founded in Europe by Gomringer. It was he who defined the new poem as a functional object. He sees in the reduction of language an achievement of great flexibility and freedom of communication. (See the manifesto *From Line to Constellation* Switzerland 1954.)

83 Brazilian. 'Terremoto' (Earthquake), a figured acrostic to be read simultaneously in several directions. Augusto de Campos 1957. From *Noigandres* no 5 1962

Together with his brother Haraoldo and with Decio Pignatori, de Campos brought out in Brazil almost synchronistically with Gomringer in Switzerland, the *Pilot Plan for Concrete Poetry*, for a poetry which would communicate its own structure, 'no longer interpreting exterior objects and/or more or less subjective feelings . . . With the concrete poem occurs the phenomenon of metacommunication, coincidence and simultaneity of verbal and non-verbal communication . . . aiming at the least common multiple of language.' (*ovo*=egg, *novelo*=ball of thread, *novo*=new, *sol*=sun, *letra*=letter (of alphabet), *estrela*=star, *soletra*=(it) spells, *so*=only, *terremoto*=earthquake, *temor*=fear, *morte*=death, *metro*=meter, *termometro*=thermometer.)

84 German. Nicht nur / informieren / haltungen / provozieren (Not only / to inform / but to provoke / attitudes). Claus Bremer in *Futura* no 8 1966

85 German. Love is a bitter mystery. Type rendered by Hansjörg Mayer.
Reinhard Döhl in *Futura* no 4 1965

86 English. 'Om Mani Pad me Hum', Buddhist mantra by Robin Greer 1965

87 French. 'Osmose Cosmos.'
Ilse and Pierre Garnier *Prototypes, Textes pour une Architecture*

88 Japanese. 'Door, Obscurity, Sound.' Seiichi Niikuni in *Anthology of Concretism*
ed. Wildman (*Chicago Review*) 1967

89 French. 'Homage to Dada' by Henri Chopin 1965

90 English. 'Sonic Water' 1964.
Dom Sylvester Houédard *op and kinkon poems* 1965

91 English. 'Tours de Babel Changée en Ponts' Free standing screens, by John
Furnival 1964-65

92 Italian. 'Spazio' by Arrigo Lora Totino 1966

93 English. 'Poem for Rosemarie', kinetic poem by Charles Cameron 1965.
Les Lettres no 34

94 Russian. Tree, made from random letters, by Valerian Neretchnikov

95 German. Poster by Ferdinand Kriwet 1964.　　　　　　　Wild Hawthorn Press

96 German. 'Allegorical Essay for Albert Wigand' by Carlfriedrich Claus 1965.
Dresdner Kupferstitch-Kabinett

97 American. 'Mirror Field inside Random Field' by Carl Fernbach-Flarsheim
1966.　　　　　*Anthology of Concretism* ed. Wildman (*Chicago Review*) 1967

98 German. 'Stuttgart' by Franz Mon.
Ainmal nur das alphabet gebrauchen edition hans jörgmayer 1967

99 English. 'Whisper Piece', a sound poem by Bob Cobbing 1969

100 Austrian. 'Zeichen' by Heinz Gappmeyr.
Chicago Review

The texts in this final section have been arranged in accordance with
Gomringer's constellation about silence, till the word, increasingly diminished,
is finally squeezed off the page by Gappmeyr.

The Second De Stijl manifesto, written in 1920, anticipated the Concrete
Poetry Movement by its proclamation:
THE WORD IS DEAD . . .
THE WORD IS IMPOTENT
asthmatic and sentimental poetry
the 'me' and 'it'
                  which is still in common use
                  everywhere . . .
is influenced by an individualism fearful of space
                  the dregs of an exhausted era . . .
psychological analysis
and clumsy rhetoric
have KILLED THE MEANING OF THE WORD . . .
the word must be reconstructed
                  to follow the SOUND as well as
                  the IDEA
if in the old poetry
                  by the dominance of relative and
                  subjective feelings
the intrinsic meaning of the word is destroyed
we want by all possible means
                  syntax
                  prosody
                  typography
                  arithmetic
                  orthography
to give new meaning to the word and new force to expression
the duality between prose and poetry can no longer be maintained
thus for the modern writer form will have a directly spiritual
meaning
it will not describe events
it will not *de*scribe at all
but ESCRIBE
it will recreate in the word the common meaning of events a constructive
unity of form and content . . .
Leiden, Holland, April 1920.
Theo van Doesburg
Piet Mondriaan
Anthony Kok
(translated by Mike Weaver)

101   England. Grave stone, Godstone.
       Photo by Aminta Barton

Acknowledgments

I should like gratefully to acknowledge Asa Benveniste of Trigram Press, who originally inspired this book, and further, the consistently helpful staff of the British Museum, both the keepers and librarians, particularly those of the Oriental Students' Room.

Since all the material was found by chance in unexpected places, I could not have carried out the research without the help of librarians, keepers and lecturers from the School of African and Asiatic Studies, the India Office Library, the Jewish Museum, the Royal Asiatic Society, the Victoria and Albert Museum and the Warburg Institute.

The modern section could not have been completed without the assistance of Robin Greer, Bob Cobbing, Peter Mayer and Edward Lucie-Smith.

Especial thanks to Bishop Toumayan, Zvia Mayroze, Miss J. R. Watson, V. J. Anand and Asmé Serajuddin for translations; to Judith Morris for her typing to Gerry Wilson for the quality of his interest and to my husband, Norman Bowler, for his persistent support and continuous encouragement.

The poem 'Axe Shape' by Dylan Thomas from *Vision and Prayer* Part II is reprinted from his *Collected Poems* by permission of J. M. Dent & Sons and the Trustees for the Copyrights of the late Dylan Thomas.

ℽ